PROFOUND HEALING *for*

Indigo

Children & Youth

...and Other Sensitive Souls

RÉMI THIVIERGE, M.S.W., R.S.W., R.M.F.T.

Profound Healing for Indigo Children & Youth...
and Other Sensitive Souls

ISBN: 978-0-9780357-1-6

Published by Phoenix Vision Publications.
#502 – 2075 Comox Street, Vancouver, B.C.
Canada, V6G 1S2
www.dynamicharmony.com.

To contact Phoenix Vision directly, call our Customer Care Department.
Toll Free: 888-FIRE007 (within Canada and US), call (604) 662-7837, or e-mail: info@dynamicharmony.com.

Acknowledgments

No book such as this, which attempts to expand the borders of our knowledge, stands on its own. I wish to thank the following for making this book possible.

Any errors in this book are my own. The strengths of the book would not have been possible without the following:

I thank Spirit and my inner guides, without whose guidance I would not have been able to provide the healing work and training that I do, or write this book. I thank them for guiding me through my career and bringing me wonderful clients to work with.

I thank my indigo son, Ben, who's been a great teacher for me.

I thank the many indigo children, youth, young adults, and their families that I've worked with over the years. I thank the many sensitive clients I've worked with. There are those whom we help, and there are those we learn from. I also thank the homeless men I've worked with, as well as clients and communities I did healing work with overseas - in Sri Lanka after the tsunami, in India with the lowest caste, and with women and children who lost everything in Haiti as a result of the earthquake in 2010. They've broadened my horizons.

I thank the following for editing all or part of my book: Suzanne Benson, Antonina Bureacenco, Diana Cawood, Michelle DeMello, Pat Lind, Karen Opas-Lanouette, and Esther Sarlo. I thank Michelle Pfeiffer for the artwork and book cover. I thank Nicole Sudom for formatting my book and taking it through the self-publication process. I thank Susanna Puppato and Carla Rieger for their wise consultation regarding my book.

The material from the following fields have been invaluable for me: child development, psychology, social work, family therapy, literature on adult children of alcoholics, mind-body healing, research on trauma, research on effectiveness of psychotherapy, psychopathology, literature regarding abuse and neglect, indigo children, parenting, energy psychology, spiritual development from the West, and spiritual and healing literature from the East, particularly from India, Tibet, and China.

Contents

Preface

So many sensitive souls are negatively impacted by having grown up and lived in unhealthy environments. Some of these very sensitive souls are indigo children, youth, and adults. Their main characteristics are that they're highly intelligent, intuitive, sensitive, and strong-minded. The central goals of this book are to assist these sensitive souls and their families to expand their understanding, experience profound healing, and raise their vibration, so that they may live with greater joy and abundance, and share their gifts more fully with the world.

My strong conviction is that all of us, but especially old souls, indigos, and other sensitive souls, can do a great deal to help heal the world. Parents of indigo children can greatly help them to do their share. If we or our children ignore the calling of our soul to heal more and more and to help others, we pay by suffering from mental, emotional, physical and relationship difficulties.

Our main focus will be on multi-dimensional transformation – on how to resolve blocks and limitations that can affect us from a variety of sources, including such areas as limiting beliefs that we carry from our ancestors, unresolved issues that we carry mentally and emotionally from our childhood, from past lives, and more. You'll learn how to do this for yourself, your loved ones, and the world around you.

We'll begin this book with a questionnaire as to what is an indigo. We'll then focus on various levels of soul development and how old souls and indigos fit within that. Following that, we'll discuss common healing methods by the traditional medical and psychiatric and psychological establishments that often don't work with indigos and other sensitive souls. We'll then focus on various types of healing methods for a variety of types of difficulties, including such issues as depression and anxiety that have proven to be very effective for many indigos and other sensitive souls. I'll then discuss how to work with various types of difficult behaviors in indigos. The next section will discuss how to quickly resolve negativity that impacts indigos and other sensitive souls that most people consider to be very difficult if not impossible to resolve, if they acknowledge these at all. I'll then give you a brief slice of the connection between indigo children and their families as they relate to very early bonding. Finally, I'll discuss the fact that indigos and old souls must develop a focus of helping the world rather than focus on their own needs if they're to remain healthy. I give as an example the healing project we've been developing in Haiti.

Who I Am and Why I've Written this Book

As of this writing, I've been in the helping field for 35 years. My first work was with young people, in a group home for youth who were out of control. We helped to stabilize them, usually over the course of a few years of treatment or more, using such methods as logical consequences and basic counseling skills. Most of them benefited. Then we sent them home. Since the parents hadn't learned to parent differently, the situations for many of the families fell apart again within a few months. I was very unsatisfied with this result, went to graduate school and, following that, received a further five years of training in family therapy. This allowed me to become certified as a family therapist and trainer with the American and Canadian Association for Marriage and Family Therapy, the accrediting body in this field. I then provided training to many psychologists, counselors, healers, and others.

Beginning around 1985, I began working with very sensitive youth who were deeply affected by the negativity around them. Two young people in particular come to mind who were very destructive. I had no idea how to help them, even with the guidance of some of the best family therapy consultants in North America.

And then my son Ben was born in 1990. He showed me from day one that I still had a great deal to learn about being a human being and a healthy parent. His great sensitivity and acting out pushed me to try many different things to see what would work best. He was eventually labeled as having ADHD – attention deficit and hyperactivity disorder.

As it turned out, Ben, as well as the other youth mentioned above, were indigos. As I learned over time, the four main characteristics of indigos are that they're very intelligent, intuitive, sensitive, and strong-minded.

I, and the helping field I work in, had no idea how to help those youth, and most still don't. The easiest thing was to label and medicate them, or to use such methods as behavior management to control them. Labeling them took our responsibility as parents off our shoulders. Obviously, if our child has a medical problem, the difficulties have nothing to do with us as parents or professionals. Or do they?

Rather than blame my son or anybody else for his difficulties, I went more deeply into myself and healed old wounds that I'd been carrying. I'd been seeing a variety of counselors and healers, as well as meditating and doing yoga since 1969, but Ben pushed me to go further. I didn't have much choice. His behavior at times had too big an impact on me to focus just on him. My personal healing work greatly improved our relationship over time and helped my son to be more settled and balanced. Talk about humility – I was at the top of my field, with the highest credentials available in family therapy, and I had to go further and deeper to learn how to deal with my son.

As I became more fully connected with my spirit, intuition, and personal power, more and more indigo children came to work with me. It was sink or swim. Indigos and other very sensitive souls have been my best teachers. Youth and families that were impossible for me to help I now find much easier to work with, and most take only a handful of sessions to resolve. More complex cases take longer. Some types of difficulties require other types of healing work from other practitioners, such as naturopaths, homeopaths, etc.

I've learned over time that the parents' inner state is crucial because our children are affected negatively if you're carrying unresolved issues from the past, are depressed, anxious, overwhelmed, angry, medicated and dull, in a power struggle with your mate, living in a negative neighborhood, drinking too much, or just plain too busy. Indigo kids are even more affected than others by these issues because they're so sensitive.

I also learned that it's essential for us as parents to learn how to help resolve what is usually thought of as negative or dark energies around and inside of our children. This is a useful view although it creates a perspective of life as being a battlefield. Actually, if we think of everything in the universe as being part of God, the Creator, All-That-Is, then it's more useful to think of "negative energies" as being lessons and helpful energies that give us an opportunity to grow rather than seeing them as being negative or destructive. There's a saying that goes, "For everything that has happened, thank you. For everything yet to come, yes."

When our children are old enough, it's important for us to teach them how to transform the negativity in their energy field and heal themselves. We and they can also learn to use positive energies to help us move forward – whether that's through connecting with our Higher Self, Soul, Full Self Potential, God, Goddess, Archangels, or what have you. The goal is to gradually go toward a place of greater and greater peace, unconditional love, and personal power. As we learn and expand, we can then more easily transform limiting beliefs and energies, and create a richer life for ourselves and our loved ones, and to help ease the suffering of others

As we learn and expand more and more, adults, children, and youth who are interested can learn to assist others to heal.

We as parents also need to take time to connect with our indigo children more positively and to bounce ideas around with them on how we both might become better world citizens and serve the world more fully. They need this from us. We can then assist them along on their path when they need our help. And maybe they could even give us feedback on ours as well.

I remember fondly that one of the consequences I gave my son when he was younger was to go pick up litter in the community. We did this as a team. I didn't think of the connection at the time, but he'd been interested in science from about age four, and later decided to study environmental studies at university. He's now thinking of becoming a politician to help improve the environment. We discuss the environment and exchange ideas on how we can both help the environment more fully. When we holiday together, we both love to go on sea kayaking adventures. When we spent time together in southern California last Christmas holiday, we agreed to take the bus in our explorations rather than rent a car. He also reminds me to turn the lights off and other such things, when I forget. My son, my teacher.

However, the turbulence and guidance I receive from Spirit is my best teacher. I need to keep being open to learn, grow, and take responsibility for whatever happens, rather than judge, hate, hide, run away, become depressed, or medicate. I ask for guidance, open and surrender, take further steps into the unknown, and ask for guidance again. That's been my best guide of all.

Perhaps you can do the same, if you're not doing so already. All turbulence, from whatever source, including our indigos, is fuel for further growth. No wonder some people call this Earth School. No wonder so many people prefer to just medicate or watch TV.

The Context

Humanity has been gradually evolving and is taking strong leaps forward in consciousness, especially in the last few decades. As many people have reported, and many of you have noticed, there's a quickening happening. Life is speeding up.

We need to clean up our lives more and more, if we want to keep up. One of the results of this quickening is that children are becoming more sensitive and, as a result, are more seriously affected by toxic environments, whether in terms of pollution or negative relationships at home, at school, or in their community.

As the vibration rises around us, our lives speed up. This brings our unresolved issues to the surface to be healed. Because they avoid dealing with their pain or don't know how to do it, more and more people are taking medication for anxiety and depression as a way of coping with the increased energy on earth. And this is why many others get divorced, only to find that "wherever you go, there you are."

The change in vibration around us is also partly why so many people no longer use what they see as rigid structures and beliefs, such as typical patriarchal relationships, old religious beliefs, traditional psychotherapy, and medical practices that disempower. People want wise advice and guidance on how they can improve their lives, rather than being told what to do.

Many of us instead are moving toward a vibrant spirituality that helps us feel closer to Spirit, along with alternative healing approaches that make it possible for us to be in charge of our own lives. More and more ancient healing modalities from all over the world, as well as new healing methods, are now available to us. What an exciting time to be alive!

Primary school teachers tell me that far more young children have special needs now than children did even ten years ago. And it was even higher then, than ten years before that, and so on. Our children are paying for our plundering and polluting Mother Earth so extensively and for our living unhealthy lifestyles.

Indigo Children in an Unhealthy Environment

Many people have been talking about very special children over recent years, especially since the first book about indigo children came out in 1999. Authors on this topic generally state that most indigos started being born in 1983, although there were some indigos prior to that. Indigos are highly intelligent, intuitive, sensitive, and strong-minded. Many writers have also commented on the variety of psychic and healing gifts that these children have.

Many people believe that indigos have come to break down old structures, such as rigid school systems, and help transform the world. However, the reality is quite different than this ideal – so far. Yes, many things have changed in our society over the last decade or so, although little of those have been initiated by the indigo children themselves – so far. Some changes have occurred to specifically accommodate the unique needs of these children.

So far, most systems that work with children have remained pretty much the same as they were a number of decades ago, with a little tinkering here and there.

Because traditional schools don't meet the needs of many kids, there's a great deal more home schooling taking place and increasing numbers of children attending independent schools. From what I've seen, it's a common pattern for many indigos to leave the traditional school system because it doesn't work for them. Some leave willingly, others are medicated or suspended after acting out.

Some teachers do attempt to make positive changes to meet the needs of these sensitive children and have wonderful success at doing so, but they work within a rigid system and are bound by the status quo.

Most school boards hold on to the old ways of teaching, even though they don't meet the needs of many of the children they're supposed to serve. I personally know a school trustee who's continually frustrated by her inability to make changes that would benefit the children, because the old guard dominates the school board. These people will get voted out in twenty years and a new breed will replace them. However, many children, and perhaps yours as well, will be deprived and suffer in the process.

A major part of this problem of change coming too slowly to meet the needs of indigos and other sensitive children is that most parents are too busy to get involved. They don't have the time that it will take to address their concerns with school officials or meet with other parents whose children are also struggling, in order to help create the changes that their children need. Others who would like to be part of the solution don't know how to proceed, or are afraid that it's too much for them to do on their own.

Many indigos in their teens and twenties, or even older, choose to opt out of the traditional work world, preferring to do their own thing instead. All too many simply think that school sucks. Many older indigos feel that what they would have to face in the work world isn't worth the effort.

The problem regarding change for the better exists not only within the school system. In most families, both parents work hard to make ends meet, although many are far more focused on their material comforts and on cocooning than on their own overall well-being or their children's. One symptom of this is the rampant rate of obesity across North America. Another is the excessive use of TV and other electronic devices, including the internet. Yet another is that far fewer people do volunteer work than was the case twenty years ago.

Family breakdown is now far more common than a few decades ago, with an increase in single-parent and blended families. Many single parents are overwhelmed by their responsibilities. Research has shown that the most significant difficulty in blended families is related to parenting. If you're interested in research on these issues, you can go to my website that focuses on family breakdown at www.intothefire.ca.

Both the children's and the family's difficulties usually increase when there's an indigo child in a single-parent or blended family because many indigos react negatively to the difficulties, whether it's through acting out, getting sick as a result of stress, or other difficulties.

In short, our children suffer, and indigos more than most, because of their acute sensitivities. They suffer because the environment is sick because we keep polluting it, because the school system is not meeting their needs, and because their parents don't have the time and energy to adequately meet their unique needs for connection and meaning. As a result, their guides become their peer group. Although youth need to spend time together, they do not have the wisdom to guide each other to lead healthier lives. They need their parents and other adults for that.

One of the concerns here is that many indigos want to help out in the world but don't know what to do or how to go about it. As a result, they can become very dissatisfied with life and their energies become misdirected. Others don't know how to channel their energies and make the best use of their gifts. Others battle the powers that be to try to improve things, whether at home, school, or work, often getting labeled negatively in the process. They're angry or depressed because what we've created feels very unhealthy to them, and they react accordingly. Some angry indigos lash out, while others are affected by our toxic environment and end up with attention deficit disorder and other serious problems.

We then label many of these sensitive and gifted children as being unhealthy because of their reactions to a negative environment and try to medicate them or use behavior management methods, instead of finding out what they need. All too often, we focus on their minds and their behavior and ignore their emotions and their spirit, as many of us ignore our own emotions and spirit. Educational systems generally do the same, although there are exceptions, such as efforts to teach children about emotional intelligence.

At the same time as most of us are ignoring our emotions and spirit, the world is speeding up and becoming spiritualized. Increased numbers of people are opening up to their spiritual side. However, this hasn't yet affected the parenting of many of us, nor our treatment of Mother Earth.

The Purpose of this Book

This book provides a positive alternative to current treatment methods by focusing on the spirit and strengths of indigos and other sensitive souls, to assist them to profoundly and quickly heal. Others, who have experienced more extensive difficulties, may need additional in-depth work than can be obtained in this book.

Once these indigos' difficulties are resolved to a fair degree, they will then be able to assist in creating a better world. Their involvement in helping to create a better world will, in turn, help them to feel even better about themselves and being in the world. The result is less avoidance of life, depression, drug consumption, crime, and suicide.

The first thing we need to do as helper/healer for our sensitive children and youth is to take steps towards attaining a higher level of functioning ourselves as parents, teachers, and professionals. As Mahatma Gandhi said, "Be the change you want to see in the world." And as the Dalai Lama said, "We can never obtain peace in the world if we neglect the inner world and don't make peace within ourselves."

Given this, one of the primary goals of this book is to assist indigos and their parents to function at higher levels, enabling them to acknowledge and offer more of their gifts to the world.

This book is also written for other sensitive souls overall. I've worked with many sensitive adults who've struggled for years, and the traditional helping world in the West wasn't able to help them because most professional helpers focus only on their clients' minds and behavior, while largely ignoring their emotions and their spirit. What we must do is focus on healing our pain at the emotional and spiritual levels and take charge of our lives in a healthy way, and not just keep on learning how to cope better in an unhealthy world.

Although I don't address this directly, this book is also meant for helping professionals and lay counselors who want to help indigos and other sensitive souls more effectively. We helping professionals have too often been part of the problem by labeling sensitive souls who suffer because of the unhealthy world we've helped to create.

I have complete conviction that for us to heal fully and reach our vast potential as human beings, we need to see ourselves as multi-dimensional beings who must heal issues that come up at all levels, from the cellular, the personality, and the relationship levels, up to the soul level and beyond. As we heal those issues more and more, we can live vastly more abundant lives and play significant roles in helping to heal the world.

Finally, our goals in my view are to serve and help to ease people's suffering as we heal our own wounds more and more. Our hearts and our spirit gradually open more and more as we go. In the end, the bottom line is to serve Spirit and to gradually go closer and closer to the Godhead. To become more and more full with Spirit, until we eventually become one with God. Put that in your own terms. It makes no difference if you believe in God or not. As an example of this, the Dalai Lama tells us that we are healthier – physically, emotionally, and in our relationships – if we focus on the well-being of others and of Mother Earth.

This book is divided into the following sections: a questionnaire on indigos, a section on soul development, methods to heal various types of difficulties, and a brief section on family-related issues.

CHARACTERISTICS OF INDIGOS: AN ASSESSMENT TOOL

The following is an overview of my perspective of the characteristics of indigo children, youth, young adults, and adults that can be used to help you determine whether you, your child, or your client is an indigo. It will also help determine whether you're a sensitive soul. Please check the following points, which may apply to the person you are assessing:

I) Highly Intelligent

☐ Ability to grasp complex matters very quickly

☑ Highly intelligent in many areas, although they may have learning disabilities

☐ Very creative

☑ Prefers to find their own path to resolving problems as opposed to following others' ideas

II) Spiritual Intelligence

☑ Has a wisdom that is beyond their age

☑ More connected with Spirit than most people

☑ Has strong empathy toward other people, animals, and the earth (although can be cold and callous if closed down emotionally)

☐ Psychic abilities, such as ability to see the aura, remember past lives, etc.

☑ Very intuitive - they know things that others don't

III) Highly Sensitive

☐ To negativity from other people, such as anxiety, anger, or depression

☐ To unhealthy foods, such as red dye, white flour, and white sugar

☐ To negative energy in their environment, such as pollution, power lines, and unhealthy communities where there's poverty and crime

☐ To conflict between people

☐ Many are uncomfortable or unhappy being in this life

☐ Emotionally sensitive, reacting more strongly than others

☐ Tendency to give up or act out

☐ May have strong allergies

☐ Needs parents and teachers to be emotionally healthy and stable

☑ May have a diagnosis of ADD (attention deficit disorder) or ADHD (attention deficit and hyperactivity disorder)

IV Very Strong-Minded

☑ Independent - does poorly with authority figures that are too laid back or controlling. Needs to be treated with respect as an equal

☐ Unwilling to perform certain duties

☐ Resists conformity - doesn't want to be the same as others

☑ Refuses to do some things and is prepared to stand up for oneself

☑ Is usually willing to express what they see even if it gets them in trouble

☐ Expresses anger toward authority figures and others if they feel the situation is unjust or if they feel pushed inappropriately

☐ Responds better to discipline if they help set up the rules and consequences

☐ Parenting them with guilt or shame doesn't work

☑ Strong integrity - only does what feels right for them

☐ May be labeled as oppositional defiant disorder

V) Social Issues: Friends, School, Work

☑ Prefers to be alone unless they're with someone similar to them (like-spirited, as opposed to like-minded)

☑ It works poorly for them to sit and be quiet in school all day

☐ May act out more than other children at home or school

☐ Refuses to do repetitive assignments

☐ Becomes frustrated by fixed structures that attempt to

get them to conform

☐ Gets bored quickly with repetitive tasks

☐ Short attention span unless focused on something they really want to do

☐ May have big ideals, but gets frustrated easily by roadblocks and is often not interested in taking the small steps required to bring their ideals to fruition

☑ Shuts down easily if tasks are too difficult, or does not feel valued.

The person being assessed is almost certainly an indigo if they score strongly in these five main categories, although they may have suppressed some of their gifts, or their gifts may have been dulled if they're on medication.

An indigo has at least 30 of these 38 attributes. Those with a score of 24 to 29 are what have been called "light workers."

Those who aren't strong in all five categories are what Doreen Virtue has called "indigos in training." Those who can relate to at least half of these factors can be thought of as "light workers." Also, sensitive souls who are not indigos would score high on sensitivity and much lower on strong-mindedness.

In my experience from working with many families with indigos, at least one parent, but likely both, also have a great deal of capacity although most are not as advanced as their child.

This tool is still being refined, as are other tools to assess indigos in other books or websites. Please contact us if you have questions or suggestions.

PART I:

FOUNDATION FOR UNDERSTANDING INDIGOS

Chapter 1
Introduction

Interestingly, at the same time as the churches have experienced the loss of many members in their congregations, research has shown that people have been doing less and less volunteer work for all types of groups, whether affiliated with a religious organization or not. This research is discussed in "The Cultural Creatives" by Paul Ray and Sherry Anderson. Hence, increasing numbers of people are developing a narrower perspective, focusing primarily on their own needs and those of their loved ones, i.e., cocooning. They've become more and more isolated and smaller in the process.

At the same time, there's an expansion in consciousness, with more people seeking to develop more of their capacity. This has included a great interest in an ever-expanding menu of methods for personal growth. It has also included an increased interest in indigos and other children with great capacity.

Literature and films about indigo children, youth, and adults created since the first book on this topic was published in 1999 have provided valuable information about these very special souls. Because the topic is so new, much of the material has tended to present a very idealized picture of what indigos are like. However, many parents don't see their special children as being quite so ideal. In fact, many experience them as being quite difficult. As a result, many parents of indigos have come to believe that their children are not indigos at all, but simply over-sensitive, troubled, or worse.

As a healer and family therapist with extensive experience working with troubled indigos and their families, I know that they have important gifts to bring to the world, but often not as much as is presented in indigo literature and films. The reason is that their gifts are veiled by such issues as depression, anxiety, and acting out.

In order to support the healthy evolution and well-being of indigo children and youth, you as parent or other concerned adult or helping professional have the task of understanding as much as possible about these unique individuals. The same applies to other sensitive souls. Otherwise, it's all too easy to perceive them in a negative light, as do so many helping professionals who are not yet aware of their existence.

One source for your understanding is the Characteristics of Indigos questionnaire on the previous pages. It can also be found on our website at www.dynamicharmony.com in the section on indigo children.

In addition, specific chapters of this book have discussions, stories, and exercises designed to address various aspects of the indigos' and other sensitive souls' characteristics as assessed in this questionnaire. These chapters will help you to more fully understand your indigo child, how to help them blossom more fully, and how you can change yourself to help them blossom even more.

As you come to better understand these issues that limit growth, you will be able to assist indigos to perform at a higher level, making it possible for them to have a very positive impact in the world, and in the process you're doing the same for yourself. This book was designed to do just that – to assist you and your indigo to resolve the kind of difficulties that prevent all of us from functioning at higher levels of capacity.

If you're a sensitive soul using this book for your own growth, simply focus on the issues regarding indigo children as though they're your own. Although some will not apply for you, a great many will.

Chapter 2
Reincarnation and Past Lives

It's important to have an understanding of reincarnation and soul ages in order to have a clearer picture of indigos and their challenges. Let's explore these issues now. If you're not interested in these topics, simply skip this section and move to the next.

Once we incarnate as human beings, there are a number of soul ages that we go through: infant soul, followed by baby soul, young, mature, old soul, and then indigo, crystal, and rainbow soul. Just as we go through different physical phases in this lifetime – baby, young child, adolescent, mature person – each soul age builds on its previous experiences in other lifetimes.

From the perspective of reincarnation, we start out by being part of the Godhead. This means that everything begins with the Source or Unmanifest. Fragments from this Source become matter so that the Godhead may become more fully realized.

Over time, our goal as souls is to experience being all things in the material world as we progress toward more and more complexity – an amoeba, a wasp, a moose, and so on. As we journey from one stage to the next, we gather more and more capacity.

Once we evolve to the point of being in human bodies, the goal is to arrive at a place of peace with, and love of, everything. This ability results in a return to the Godhead and becoming one with God. Understanding soul ages helps put the progress towards this goal into perspective. This information will help you better understand both your indigo child and yourself.

Although some people believe that the soul is completely pure and perfect, many, including myself, believe that our soul carries karma, or luggage, resulting from our actions. For example, Jesus said, "As you sow, so shall you reap." Buddhists, Hindus, Christians up to the third century A.D., and others believe that this luggage is carried from one lifetime to another. This is our causal body, which is made up of positive and negative karma. The difficulties we suffer are either a result of working through old karma or being given lessons the soul needs to learn. Our soul gradually learns and evolves over lifetimes. Negative karma, based on our negative actions, obscures the light that can come into us, and results in our being caught up in illusion. Since indigos are more connected with their spirit than most people, some are also in touch with past lives. Some of the indigos I work with remember their past lives or feel pain where they've been wounded in previous lives. A great many indigos don't want to be bothered by little tasks in the material world. They only want to do big things. This is a direct result of their being more in touch with the goals of their soul during this lifetime. It could also be said that some indigos are confused about who they are and how they fit into the world, and so they may accomplish very little as a result.

According to Pema Chodron, a Tibetan Buddhist teacher, the journey toward enlightenment involves shedding, not collecting. It's an ongoing process of opening and surrender, the same as taking off layer after layer of clothing until we're completely naked with nothing to hide. This fits other spiritual paths as well, including Christian, Buddhist, and Hindu perspectives. We need to let go of the belief that we're this body, and instead come to see that we're fragments of God, of Spirit. To open and surrender more and more. To give our hearts to the world.

There's no guarantee that you'll reach your level of capacity as a soul in this lifetime. You have to work toward it. For example, if you're an old soul, you could live a life focused on fear and despair, and never open to the capacity that you've acquired in previous lifetimes. Or you could simply focus on your own needs and ignore the needs of others. On the other hand, it's possible to grow the equivalent of a number of lifetimes in one lifetime.

Before reincarnating into the next lifetime, souls choose whether they want to be on a slow path of growth or one with great acceleration. Those on the slower path generally choose lifetimes that are relatively peaceful. On the other hand, many of those who want the quicker path choose to be born into very difficult childhoods, where there are such difficulties as abuse, neglect, divorce, and so on. However, many souls, when making the decision about where to be born, misjudge the extent of the challenge they'll experience, and the personality ends up being overwhelmed by their life situation. The result of this is that the soul doesn't really want to be here. Because of this, there's insufficient connecting between the soul and the cells. They focus instead on trying to get to heaven or to be enlightened, or avoid in other ways, rather than bring their gifts into the world, as was intended.

In other cases, people really want to heal but they don't succeed despite their best efforts because they stay with approaches and practitioners that don't have the capacity that they need in order to heal. Practitioners can only assist us to go as far as they've gone themselves. The client's loyalty in continuing to work with methods that are insufficient prevents them from moving forward to the degree that is needed for them to fulfill their potential. How can a practitioner or a method that's not connected with Spirit or not grounded and focused on helping you to blossom, help you to expand more fully in those areas?

Others react to what they experience as a negative environment by not wanting to be here and so they participate minimally in their own lives, putting in only halfhearted efforts to deal with life. They sit on the sidelines. Some of them do this for a number of lifetimes due to unresolved issues from many previous lifetimes, e.g., self-hatred for things they've done lifetimes ago, or hatred of God for not responding when they called for help.

In order for an individual to grow as much as they can, work needs to be done on healing these types of issues at the soul level, as well as healing issues at the physical, personality, and relationship levels. Most practitioners only focus on one or two of these levels.

My experience has taught me that as healers working with indigos and other sensitive souls, we need to be able to assess and work multi-dimensionally – at a variety of levels, including cellular, DNA, mind, emotions, relationships, soul, and soul group levels. If we as helpers and healers can't work on these various levels, we'll continue to fail many indigos and sensitive souls.

Chapter 3
Soul Ages

To help you understand yourself, indigo children, and others more fully, let's explore the issue of soul ages. You don't need to believe in reincarnation or even in God for the concept of soul ages to be useful for you. Simply see them as different types of personalities, each having particular gifts and handicaps. No stage is better than another, just as being four years old is no better or worse than being twenty-seven or seventy-two.

The issues discussed here are important to understand, because indigos and other sensitive souls often remain stuck at the soul and personality levels. Both levels must be resolved for individuals to grow to their full potential.

For example, an old soul may operate as a baby soul because they're caught up in fear regarding money. To grow through this, they must let go of old survival fears at both the personality and soul levels. They also need to open and surrender, as well as move into their power. This is part of the multi-dimensional work that is illustrated throughout this book.

As an example of this, I'll tell you a bit about my own personal journey. I had been experiencing a great deal of fear for all my life, beginning as far back as I can remember. Part of the issue was that I grew up in a family where I felt I shouldn't have been born and was in the way. I worked with many helping professionals to help me heal this but made no real progress. It's only when I began exploring issues at the DNA level regarding my ancestors, as well as at the soul and soul group levels, that my fears became more and more fully resolved.

A very useful writer on the topic of soul ages is Joya Pope, who has written a book specifically on soul ages. You'll find the reference to this book as well as others that I mention in the bibliography at the end of this book. Michael Newton, author of "Journey of Souls," is also an excellent writer on this subject.

Some writers believe that there are seven phases to each of the soul ages, and that it takes one to ten lifetimes to complete each one. Other writers believe that it takes twenty to forty lifetimes to go through each soul age, whereas still others believe that we go through hundreds, if not thousands, of lifetimes.

Despite the varying perspectives on how and how fast we grow, the idea of gradual development of souls and of humanity in general is a very common one for many spiritual paths.

There's no guarantee that we'll gradually progress upwards. Buddhists and Hindus believe that it's possible for us to go back down the scale and reincarnate as animals if we're destructive in a particular lifetime. However, as the ascended master Djwhal Khul has said through Alice Bailey, and quoted by Joshua David Stone: the overall trend is that "all moves onwards and upwards." Teilhard de Chardin, a Christian writer, also has the perspective of ongoing development at all levels. This fits for nature, humanity, and the cosmos as a whole. This is also one of the fundamental laws of science. Even though we might go downhill for a time, the trend is always toward further growth.

As part of onwards and upwards evolution, indigos are said to be here to help us go forward to the next phase of the evolution of humanity. In the same way, those who assist indigos to blossom are also growing a great deal in the process. To do this, it's necessary that you "have your act together," to bring your own richness into the world in one way or another. You may do this through the conscious and loving parenting of your children, through being kind to others, or through your career or other means.

Description of Soul Ages

Each soul age brings its own gifts and challenges, both for the individuals experiencing them and others involved. Your understanding of the gifts and challenges of each soul age, but especially of old soul and indigo soul ages, will be of great benefit for you to assist your indigo child to function at their highest capacity. This map will also be of great benefit to help you move forward in your own life.

Old souls have been a subject of discussion for a number of years, and more recently, you may have heard about crystal and rainbow children. You may also have occasionally heard about bodhisattvas. What does all this mean?

The following is a summary of these various soul ages beginning with the youngest. One soul age is not better than the others and each has its particular strengths and weaknesses. We all have unresolved issues from childhood, as well as from earlier soul ages. In addition, we carry historical trauma in our DNA from our ancestors, along with negativity from our relationships as adults and our environment.

Just as we carry old vestiges of the brains of more primitive life forms such as our limbic brain, also known as the lizard brain, which deals with fight, flight, or freeze, we also carry old vestiges of earlier soul ages. These influences are very powerful. For example, it's easy for us to get stuck in such issues as being overly loyal to our clan to the detriment of our personal growth, fear of not having enough money, and fear of suffering and of dying.

As you read this, think about where you and your indigo child might fit and what phase their soul might still be stuck at. This will help you clarify the potential challenges, as well as potential solutions that you might not have previously considered.

Infant Souls

The main issue for infant souls to focus on is survival – to learn how to survive on earth. They live with many fears.

It's said that there is only a small percentage of infant souls in North America and other developed countries at this time. Most infant souls are reportedly born in countries around the equator, usually in tribal conditions. The reason for this is that it's easier to survive there, although they're faced with a variety of additional difficulties, such as hurricanes, poisonous snakes, malaria, and other diseases.

These souls are still very closely connected to Spirit, more so than the older soul ages, but not more so than indigos. They resonate closely with the earth and have learned to live in profound harmony with nature. As with babies, infant souls live in the moment, not planning for the future, which is different than later soul ages. This is similar to the way babies and young children live in the moment.

Infant souls tend to be very earthy and intuitive, but without a deep mental understanding of the complexities of life. They focus on conformity or oneness with their group or tribe rather than on personal growth. They're deeply threatened if a member of the group wants to question or explore different beliefs and approaches.

Think of when you've been insecure in your life. We tend to try to conform and want others to conform more at those times, just as infant souls do. The term for this is regression – going back to a younger age.

There are seven energy centers that run from the bottom of the spine to the top of the head, called chakras. The first center, at the base of the spine, relates to conformity with our clan, survival issues, and connection with the earth. The stability of the clan is more important than the individual's needs or growth at this phase. Therefore, the infant soul age corresponds to the first chakra, the energy centre at the base of the spine.

See the exercise below on how to identify and work with these issues to transform fear and other negative emotions.

Research described by Mona Lisa Schulz in "Awakening Intuition," a very useful book, has described a great deal of medical research showing that there's a strong correlation between each chakra being open or closed and particular personality characteristics, which also correlate with specific illnesses. For example, people with a heart chakra that is too open or too closed are more likely to have illnesses in that physical area, such as heart conditions and breast cancer.

Modern Western society is very destructive to the earth specifically because most of us have lost our connection with Mother Earth. We must transcend old issues such as this if we want to continue growing.

Exercise:

Think of old fears you may have, of being alone, of not having enough money, of being rejected, or of dying. Imagine light going into the seat of your soul, which is six inches (15 centimeters) above the top of your head and burning away old issues relating to this at the soul level.

Imagine light going into your first chakra, at the

> *base of your spine, and cleansing old fears from there. Also do this at the cellular level in the DNA – transforming old ancestral fears.*
>
> *Try this exercise for at least ten minutes.*

If you're a parent of an indigo, you can then teach this to your child. If your child is too young to do it or if your child is unmotivated or closed to healing work, you can visualize it for them. Ask Spirit to go down to the various levels to do this work. It's not necessary for you to believe in God or Spirit to do these exercises. Some Buddhists, for example, use the elementals. They use visualizations such as imagining rain or sunshine coming down, for example.

When you do this exercise, as well as the others mentioned in this book, you can expect to feel lighter. Some people will not feel a change even though the exercises are helpful for them because they're not in touch with their own energy. Many of those people are also not in touch with their own emotions. They're closed to their own experience. Others will not succeed in doing this and other exercises because they have blocks that prevent them from succeeding. I suggest you work at transforming these blocks with some of the exercises provided in the next section. If it still doesn't work, I recommend you work with an intuitive healer. You can find one locally or contact us if you still don't make progress.

Another form of block to experiencing success with these exercises is being on medication.

> ### Story:
>
> *As an example, I recently worked with a 13-year-old indigo and his parents, one of whom was a professor. They were concerned about their son smoking marijuana. He had previously been anorexic, depressed, and suicidal. A psychiatrist had him hospitalized and put him on medication. The strong medication he was on resulted in his not being able to feel the results of the healing work I was doing with him even though I could feel the negative energy coming out of him. He's a very sensitive soul with a great deal of capacity to heal quickly, but the medication he was on closed him to his experience.*

Baby Souls

As with small children, the main issue that baby souls have to learn is to deal with discipline and order. Baby souls need the security of someone imposing a structure on them and telling them what to do. Both baby and infant souls have difficulty understanding abstract concepts and may have difficulty with school for that reason. They're more holistic and concrete rather than being able to think in abstract terms, such as mathematics or science.

As we'll see later, indigos are able to be abstract as well as having a very strong holistic sense. However, they tend to be much more right-brained and creative than left-brained, which specializes in linear thinking. As a result, some have difficulty with traditional forms of education.

Although baby souls are more sophisticated than infant souls, they still need to work at resolving a great many fears. Survival has mostly been worked out at this phase and there's a beginning focus on self-development. It's like a two-year-old child walking away from a parent and standing up for himself, while at the same time staying close by and trying to follow the rules.

Baby souls see anyone who's different from them as being bad – whether it's a different religion or another culture, among other things. There's an "in group" as opposed to an "out group." As we all know, elementary school children often act out these issues by attacking children who are different from them.

When we're younger, we briefly experience younger soul ages, and so these children, even if they're old souls or indigos, are acting out baby soul mentality and behavior for a number of years. It's basically like going through lessons that we've learned in previous lifetimes, until we eventually grow to the level of our capacity. As an example of that, an old soul goes through phases through each life of acting like an infant, baby, young, and mature soul, before growing into its capacity as an old soul.

The pattern of in and out crowds results in many indigos getting picked on and bullied at school because many of them dress or behave differently from others. As another example, my son was teased at school in the early grades for being too intelligent. He shut down his mental capacity for some years because of that.

Many people are advanced souls but stick to security as if they were infant and baby souls because of unresolved childhood fears or unresolved karma, as well as carrying unresolved issues at the DNA level from previous generations.

As an example, a close friend of mine has a great deal of capacity as a healer. However, she keeps getting little jobs in child care, which she outgrew many years ago. As a result, Spirit gives her the message over and over that she shouldn't be there through disagreements with parents, being kicked by the children, and so on, even though she's quite lovable. She's a big spirit trying to hide and be small, and she keeps getting in trouble for it. This is an example of using our will and ignoring messages from the universe.

Do you know anyone like that? How about yourself? Are you using your potential, or avoiding it like the plague? As Nelson Mandela said, we're most afraid of our light, not our darkness.

Infant and baby souls are prepared to follow any strong, confident leader who gives them a black and white view of life. We can hope that they'll follow positive leaders, although they just as easily could follow ones with evil intent, such as Khomeini, Hitler, or others who tell them that they're fighting for God and eliminating evil.

Infant and baby souls are extremely dogmatic and, as with the leaders mentioned above, can be quite brutal with those who disagree with them or are different from them. They have the highest regard for their leaders.

Political and religious leaders can easily manipulate populations that are made up of a large proportion of infant and baby souls because of their fears and their willingness to sacrifice their lives for eternal glory through suicide bombings and other means. Interestingly, the point has been raised that some indigos are also willing to sacrifice their lives through such means for what they see as the greater good.

Using an example closer to the home arena, when a child gets in trouble with an authority figure, baby soul parents will get their child to obey the authority figure rather than support their child's concerns, even when the child is in the right. Older souls can do this as well if they've learned to be in fear of authority, because they're traumatized, or because they're depleted due to issues such as illness or exhaustion.

Baby souls are unable to see how they're part of the problem when they're in difficulty. It's far easier to blame the other side, take a drug, or attack, than deal with one's own feelings and imperfections. Young souls, to be discussed next, are also unable to take responsibility for their actions.

The following story gives you an example of my work with infant and baby souls.

Story:

I did some volunteer work with a group of "untouchables" in India at the end of 2008. They're people who are considered to be at the bottom of the social ladder, and they're seen as being only good enough to do menial, undesirable work such as sweep the streets or clean toilets. The people I worked with were gypsies, a group who are at the bottom of the untouchables class. They were rarely even given work.

It was very enlightening for me to work with them. They trusted me right away, because they saw me as an authority figure. I could have taken advantage of them and controlled them very easily because they were so naïve and trusting, and because of their need for a strong leader who tells them what to do. This gets infant and baby souls into trouble regularly, electing politicians who are bullies to be in control of their lives, even if many of them die in the process, or allowing multi-nationals to devastate their land rather than stand up to them.

The group I met with was very open to growing spiritually. I taught them some healing visualizations, similar to the ones I share with you in this book. They were able to benefit from them a great deal. The negativity they had been carrying for millennia was resolved. They were no longer walking with a dark cloud over their heads. As a result, they were able to get jobs more easily than was previously possible for them.

In order to assist them to be in charge of their lives, I also provided them with tools and seeds to make a garden, fishing nets, and sewing machines,

> *as well as the training to use them. This worked very*
> *well. The material "carrots" I provided attracted*
> *them to come and do the healing work. If you're*
> *interested in learning more about this project, go*
> *to www.dynamicharmony.com in the international*
> *articles section.*
>
> *I used this combination of "carrots" and healing*
> *work with homeless men in my community as well*
> *and it worked great with them too. I had initially*
> *offered them healing work and no one came. When*
> *I gave them five dollars for a half-hour session, they*
> *lined up for help – and benefited from it.*

In my view, if we want to help humanity move forward in this way, it's important for us to take steps to help the "poorest of the poor" all over the world, not just in our own communities. As Mother Teresa said, some can work directly with these people, others can give money, and others can pray for the cause.

As part of my small contribution to help humanity, I went to Haiti in June 2010 with a group of people that I trained to help to heal some of the trauma there. This was the most disadvantaged country in the Western hemisphere before the earthquake in early 2010.

When you go through the exercises below, think of this group. Ninety-five percent of them have ancestors who were slaves, some practice voodoo, and the country is run by multi-nationals and six wealthy families. Groups such as the

United Nations and the Red Cross have poured billions of dollars into Haiti with no real positive impact, because they haven't found a way to help the people deeply heal and be empowered to run their own lives.

One of my dreams in the near future is to train a group of indigos on how to help to heal trauma, and take them to Haiti and other impoverished countries in the Third World. The main goal would be to help heal infant and baby souls, who have strong spirits, as the indigos do. If you're interested in this project, have a look at www.dynamicharmony.com.

Exercise:

Imagine the light going into the seat of your soul, six inches (15 centimeters) above your head to transform judgment and the need to control others that stems from past lives. Also, do so in your DNA to resolve your ancestors' patterns of judgment and control by having light go in through the top of your head and into the core of each cell. Transform insecurities at the DNA level that you've picked up from your ancestors, resulting in the need for somebody else to manage your life for you rather than being your own authority. Imagine light going between you and other people and clearing away your judgment toward them, and their judgment toward you.

You can use these exercises to assist your indigo to heal as well. Do it for them if they're too young or unwilling to do the exercise. When doing such healing work, it makes no difference how far away they are.

You can do distance healing by imagining light going through the crown of your head to your heart center in the center of your chest. Then imagine that light going to their heart center. Next, imagine light going from above to the crown of their head. After that, imagine Spirit clearing whatever difficulty in your child you're trying to assist with. You can do this type of healing work with anyone, not just with indigos. It's very effective, unless there are other blocks that need to be resolved.

Young Souls

Young souls are testing their capacity in the world. They're spreading their wings and want to see how far they can get. They want action and don't bother with emotions or spirit, their own or anyone else's.

Young souls may use anger, lies, or manipulation to get their own way. From their perspective, the ends justify the means when it comes to advancing their personal goals. Because their central goal is to see how much they can get out of life, they often gravitate toward positions of power. Many lawyers, business people, executives, and politicians are young souls. Of course, many in those professions are also advanced souls who are doing good work in the world.

Young souls represent the most competitive soul age and that which is least positively connected to God or to other people. If someone gets run over by a young soul, the latter is likely to say, "It's their own fault – they shouldn't have been in the way." Long-term consequences resulting from acquiring power and money, such as damage to one's health or marriage or the environment, are not important. The goal is to make things happen and the niceties of life are simply irrelevant. Because young souls are so goal-oriented, they can be very industrious, and even tireless.

As Joya Pope wrote, we owe them our efficiency, our military power, and our continual striving to make things happen and change. They are the builders of civilization.

One of the aspects of young souls is that they don't let themselves be pushed around, as other soul ages do. The only exception to this is indigos, who also refuse to be pushed around. If more of us were in our power, the earth would be in far better shape than it is because we would be willing to stand up and say "no" to the destructive behavior of those in charge. Instead, the vast majority simply go along as the rich get richer and the middle class struggles more and more to get by as the earth becomes more and more devastated.

Where do you fit in this? How do you handle it when your indigo child complains that some things are really stupid or destructive? Do you encourage them to conform or to take steps to help the world become a better place?

Many of you who are reading this book have a fear of being in your power. The result is that not only the world, but your indigo child, may push you around as well. Your indigo is here not to push you around, but to teach you about being in your power.

Exercise:

Have light go into the seat of your soul, 6 inches (15 centimeters) above your head, and clear away old karma - old negative deeds that we did when we were young souls, creating damage to ourselves and others. Also do this at the level of DNA - have light go in through the top of your head into every cell in your body, and then into your DNA. Have light go in and transform our guilt and shame for having treated others so badly in the past.

Assist your indigo to heal in this way as well.

Doing this exercise on occasion over time will assist us to be more free of shame and guilt, and to come to be more and more fully in our power.

Mature Souls

As with middle-aged people, mature souls ask the big questions about life. "Why am I here? Does God exist? What happens after I die?"

The issues of money, power, and fame are no longer quite as important as they were during the young soul stage, and these issues will become even less so for old souls. Working hard to get ahead is no longer seen as being important.

Mature souls are more likely to be focused on relationships rather than on their own personal needs and concerns. There's more of a focus on helping others at this soul age, as well as at later ones.

Mature souls have more capacity to consider other people's points of view than when they were younger souls. Their emotions and relationships are the main focus of their lives. It's no longer easy to control others to accomplish their goals because guilt and shame now interfere. Mature souls feel bad if they focus only on their own well-being, while ignoring the needs of others.

Many people who are mature or old souls function at the young soul level during their early adulthood and move more into their soul capacity as they go into their forties and beyond. This is because we become more fully connected with our soul energetically once we hit mid-life, and at this point will often do a life review and ask the big questions.

Mature souls also tend to go through a great deal of drama in their relationships, trying to have things their way, rather than being at peace with others. This applies even with their spouse, trying to control them, to get them to behave in a way that they want, rather than allowing them to be who they are. This either ends up in power struggles for years or in the partners withdrawing from each other. It often ends up in divorce.

I spent years working with clients who argued a great deal about such issues as dirty socks on the floor. Most were more interested in winning than in having a happy life. When I got tired of this and asked Spirit to send me clients who really wanted to heal, my whole clientele changed to people who were willing to take responsibility for their issues.

Exercise:

Imagine that you're like a kitten all caught up in a ball of twine, but that you're also caught up there with another kitten. This is perhaps your child, mate, or boss. This image represents the entanglements between you and another person when in the mature soul age.

Have light go into the seat of your soul and transform these entanglements between you and others. Transform that from your aura as well, a meter (three feet) all around you. Also clear that at the DNA level. If you're entangled with a particular individual, imagine clearing the space between you and the other person. Ask that the negative energies be transformed from them as well. Send them love and light through your heart center, and let them know at the soul level that you'd like to be at peace and in a win-win relationship with them.

Now, assist your indigo child to transform these issues as well. It makes no difference if your child is very young. They carry these issues from birth and before that.

Doing this exercise on occasion will help you to become clearer and more spacious and loving in your relationships. Transforming issues at the infant, baby, mature, and younger soul levels will result in old souls and indigos being able to function more

> *fully at their own levels of development, rather than continuing to be limited by unresolved issues from younger levels of development, such as old fears and shame, and focusing solely on their own needs to the detriment of others.*

Old Souls

Almost everyone who will read this book is an old soul or an indigo and, for this reason, I'll discuss old souls more fully here than the earlier soul ages.

As with infant and baby souls, old souls are very connected with their spirit, although they're more complex and have a far greater mental understanding and perspective than do infant and baby souls. Old souls are generally very sensitive, although mostly not in their power. One of the aspects of this is that many old souls are highly sensitive to other people's energy, and can easily be thrown off base by it. When I speak of sensitive souls other than indigos in this book, you can think of them as mostly being old souls.

Old souls are able to have a broad perspective of everyone else's position because they've been there. While most of us have the tendency to lose our perspective when caught up in a situation, old souls can see so many sides of an issue that it can become very difficult for some of them to determine right from wrong or good guys vs. bad guys. They can be immobilized because they see so many options and are unsure about which one to take.

Old souls take much longer to reach their potential than younger souls do because they're much more complex. For example, younger souls are generally fully mature by 21 years of age. They know where they're going and what they want to accomplish. In comparison, old souls are coming into their own at age 35, if the conditions are right. Many old souls focus inward more than on accomplishing a great deal in the world.

One of the factors affecting old souls is that many have chosen very difficult situations to be born into and they're very focused on healing the resulting wounds. Many are overwhelmed by these circumstances, including such issues as historical trauma, shame, and guilt – and can't find a way to resolve them. In addition, they carry a great deal of shame, guilt, and self-hatred from having done many negative things in previous lifetimes to achieve their goals.

One consideration is that many of the helping practitioners who work with old souls don't know how to help them heal from such difficulties as shame and self-hatred because they haven't been there or haven't learned to resolve those issues thoroughly themselves.

Many old souls never reach their capacity for a variety of other reasons, such as choosing to withdraw and blame, following false gurus, staying on paths that aren't helpful for them, substance abuse, and avoiding taking full responsibility for what's going on in their lives. This makes it very easy for young souls to control the world around old souls, as it is with other soul ages, except for indigos.

Another factor affecting old souls is that because they feel incapable of or are unwilling to meet their own material needs, many female old souls choose relationships with young souls who are focused on making a great deal of money, thus providing their wives with a sense of security. However, the young soul husband ignores his wife's needs and emotions, and she eventually ends up being dissatisfied with the relationship.

Many of these female old souls end up shutting down, getting sick or depressed, or divorcing their partner. Some who remain in the relationship use it as a foundation for security and personal growth, and accept the fact that the spousal relationship is simply not fulfilling. Those who end up separating will hopefully choose more wisely next time and select a partner who matches their own soul development. However, that is often not the case. Love, passion, and our need for security can make us blind.

Old souls can often get stuck trying to come to terms with issues they've already overcome in a younger soul age, such as fears relating to money and survival, which they learned as infant souls. The universe uses money as well as other issues, such as health and relationships, to test and push us all to grow. The negative focus that many old souls develop around these issues results in their losing trust in their own abilities.

The result is that they often end up not reaching their potential. The Hindu and Buddhist perspective is that these souls will simply keep facing the same lessons, one lifetime after the other, until the lessons are mastered.

One of the main goals at the old soul stage is to focus on non-attachment – not getting caught up in the drama and intensity of life, and place less emphasis on material needs than was done at earlier stages. As a result of their non-attachment, some old souls may seem stand-offish. However, this attitude tends to result in more inner peace.

Old souls' self-esteem is often quite low, in part because others see them as being deficient for seemingly not being involved in mastering life and because they compare their own lives to the goals of a materialistic society. The issue is that they have not yet learned to fully love and surrender their lives to the universe. The old rules of creating wealth through a great deal of effort no longer work at their phase of development and they haven't yet fully come into their spiritual capacity of being able to manifest with ease.

Many old souls explore a variety of religions and teachings before settling down to one or a combination they prefer. Others keep searching throughout their lives. Some simply give up and become cynical.

Old souls have a strong focus toward inner growth and toward Spirit, and many have little interest in creating change in the world. However, they can accomplish a great deal with relatively little effort when they figure out some of the laws of the universe, such as the law of attraction. They're more likely to succeed in doing this after they resolve certain issues, such as a sense of unworthiness, that prevent this law from working for them.

Most old souls have little interest in money or fame and may become prominent only for the sake of teaching others.

Exercise:

Attachment to some things and rejection of others is a big issue for old souls to resolve. Instead of grasping and pushing things away, the goal is to be in a place of peace and non-attachment, while also having a positive impact in the world. We need to learn to take steps in the world, while surrendering the results to Spirit and leaving it to Spirit to look after us. As Christ said in the Sermon on the Mount, be as the birds and the lilies in the field. Be at peace and you'll be looked after.

Imagine coming to a place of peace at all levels rather than the old push and pull: acceptance and surrender. Remember the line from Alcoholics Anonymous that says that we need to "accept the things we cannot change and strive to resolve the ones we can, and have the wisdom to know the difference." Ask Spirit to help you to surrender your ego because its related fears, greed, distrust, and need for praise prevent us from reaching our full potential. At this level and the soul levels above it, we need to learn to say "thy will versus mine." Ask for guidance to bring your gifts into the world in the way that will be most beneficial.

Help your indigo to do this exercise. Doing this exercise regularly over time will assist us and them to

---

be less encumbered by the illusion that the material world is all there is. As we and our indigo become less caught up in these negativities, we can be more at peace and accomplish more and more positive goals in the world, with a stronger focus on making the world a better place.

Indigos

It's useful to think of the gradual evolution of soul ages as moving toward a higher vibration, just as there are lower musical notes and higher-pitched notes. For example, an old soul is of a higher vibration and is more sensitive than a young soul. In the same way, an indigo is of a higher vibration and is more sensitive than an old soul. However, the implication is that soul ages have incarnated on earth over time.

Some psychics suggest that indigos have had little experience on earth and don't quite know how to be here because their incarnational journeys have mostly been in other galaxies. They can easily feel that they don't belong in the family they're in because they're so different from other family members. At the very least, most are more evolved than their parents and siblings.

As I noted earlier, the four main characteristics of indigos are that they are very intelligent, intuitive, sensitive, and powerful. There's a great deal of variation from one indigo to the next in terms of these capacities and it would be a mistake to see them as being very similar to each other. For example, they may be very intelligent in some ways and not in others. Or, some are very powerful and others much less so, whereas others have suppressed their power.

I believe that it's only when they integrate their great talents within themselves and learn to work with others in the same general direction, such as helping with the environment, that indigos will be able to have a powerful and positive impact in the world. However, they can certainly find personal fulfillment by following their own path and doing what feels right for them.

To date, I've seen little evidence of indigos breaking down very many walls successfully in the school system and in corporations, although some schools and some teachers have developed alternative approaches that are helpful for indigos. Regretfully, these alternative approaches are often vulnerable to funding cuts because they cover more than the basic 3 Rs – Reading, Writing, and 'Rithmetic.

We, the current generation of helpers as well as those in authority, including their parents, need to learn how to harness the gifts indigos bring if we're serious about wanting to help them create a better world. At this time, most school systems in the developed world are in financial crisis because there are fewer and fewer students, partly because of fewer numbers of children, and also because so many children and indigos today are home schooled or go to alternate schools.

As the old generation of school boards is replaced, new school board members will hopefully realize the importance of thinking more collaboratively to invite the creative gifts of some of their teachers, parents, and students in order to keep more indigos and other sensitive souls in traditional schools.

For now, most if not all mainstream school systems are still dominated by a top-down, hierarchical type of thinking.

For example, in the region where I live, the Vancouver School District, only 31% of aboriginal youth completed high school, until just a few years ago. For males in general, a little over 80% complete high school. The rate is a little better for girls. These percentages apply only to the youth who remain in high school until grade 12, and do not include the many that leave the system prior to grade 12.

Indigos are usually born into families where at least one parent is an old soul. If only one of the parents is an old soul, my experience is that it's usually the mother. These parents generally fit into what has been termed "cultural creatives." This means that one or both parents have been either strongly focused on feminism, the environmental movement, personal growth, or on creating social change. This includes the growing number of people who've focused on methods of personal growth, such as meditation and yoga. A great deal of research has been done on this and is covered in "Cultural Creatives" by Paul Ray and Sherry Anderson.

In my experience, indigos and old souls are able to heal very quickly with the use of energy psychotherapy and healing by connecting with Spirit. Many of them embrace a multi-dimensional perspective, while others try desperately to suppress their gifts and be normal in order to be accepted by their peers.

Many old souls are not able to heal using such methods as healing visualizations until they're in their mid-thirties, whereas indigos, because of their greater connection with their spirit, can do so from an early age. Infant and baby souls can do so with ease, whereas young and mature souls do not have the ability to connect with their spirit through healing visualizations, in my experience. However, as I mentioned earlier, some indigos and old souls, mostly males, don't benefit from healing visualizations either. However, many sensitive males do benefit a great deal from this work.

Most indigos that I see have a high healing ability. Many have psychic gifts, such as an ability to see auras, to connect with past lives, and so on. Others are very artistic or have gifts relating to science or engineering. Others are exceptional speakers.

Most are very independent. In addition, many indigos have what we might call righteous anger. They're often intolerant toward injustice and want to see more fairness in their lives and in the world. However, some prefer to avoid pain and do not wish to see the suffering in the world. They can be intolerant and harsh with their feedback to others. Others are painfully affected by negative energy around them and withdraw. Some become involved with drugs as a way of reaching a "high" or coping with pain. They can also become aggressive or suicidal.

It's been my experience thus far that more young female indigos are more interested in healing work than are most indigo males. This is also true for other soul ages. In my experience, and that of most professional helpers I know, about 85% of counseling clients and those who attend personal growth workshops are women.

> ### Exercise:
>
> *At this point, it would be helpful for you to scan your results on the assessment tool about indigos at the beginning of this book. Determine which areas are weaker for you. You can then practice resolving those issues that block you from having these gifts more fully, and build on related strengths using the exercises provided throughout this chapter and in other parts of this book.*

Crystal Children

Because of the type of work I do, I've had very little experience with crystal children. As a result, what I write here about crystal, rainbow, and super psychic kids is based on what I've heard and read rather than from direct experience.

Indigos are sometimes mistakenly called crystal children and the crystals are also being mistakenly called indigo kids. For those of you who've seen the indigo movie from 2005, I would define that as a crystal child – not an indigo. That movie and the indigo movie presented in February 2006 both focused almost totally on the more evolved, higher functioning indigos.

Unlike indigos, many of whom have an angry edge, crystal children have a very calm temperament. They're very sensitive, as are indigos, although unconditional love and compassion are essential parts of their being. Because of their peaceful energy, they draw other people to them. They also have great healing abilities.

Indigos operate mostly from their sixth chakra, which is the third eye or intuitive center and is indigo in color. Crystals operate more from the seventh or crown chakra, the energy center at the top of our head. This chakra connects us with Spirit. They're also said to communicate telepathically and, partly for this reason, some don't bother beginning to speak until they're three to four years of age. They reportedly have a strong need to help people in difficulty. For example, parents tell me that when they're upset, their crystal children nurture them and help them heal.

Whereas indigos are said to be here to break down walls that no longer serve humanity, crystal children are here to help us connect more fully with Spirit and to learn to love unconditionally.

For those of you who are interested in crystal and other highly advanced children, I recommend you read Doreen Virtue's book on this subject. She also has a CD on this topic. You may also want to read "The Children of Now: Crystalline Children, Indigo Children, Star Kids, Angels on Earth, and the Phenomenon of Transitional Children" by Meg Blackburn Losey.

Rainbow Children

I've had no experience with these children. They've sometimes been referred to as super psychic, star, or millennium children. It's said that they can use their strong will and unlimited energy to help build the new world. The literature that focuses on these children states that there have been rainbow children on earth since the year 2000, although they may not yet have awakened to their full potential.

Unlike crystals, who open up only to those who are responsive to them, rainbows are unconditionally loving to all. Rainbow kids are said to have extremely strong wills, high energy, embrace life with enthusiasm, and are creative and passionate.

The predicted influx of rainbow children on earth will be between 2010 and 2030 as compared to between 1990 and 2010 for crystals, according to some psychics. As the reader will realize, these predictions and dates are only speculative.

Although some writers do not differentiate between the two groups, there appears to be a big difference between rainbows and super psychic kids in that the latter have extremely high psychic abilities. Many of them are reported to have been born in Russia.

The Perspective of Levels of Consciousness

It's useful to compare the soul ages to the scale of consciousness developed by David Hawkins and first presented in his book, "Power vs. Force." According to this scale, people who rate below 200, on a scale of 0 to 1,000, are not in a place of integrity or responsibility toward others. They tend to be dominated by fear, shame, guilt, and anger. Ethics are not particularly relevant at this stage. Infant, baby, and young souls fall below 200.

Above 200, people are more focused on at least trying to treat others as they would like to be treated. According to Hawkins' research, 22% of humanity falls above 200, although the proportion of this group in the United States, for example, is 49%. We can expect the proportion of that group to be about the same in other developed countries such as Canada, and to be much lower in many Third World countries.

As they evolve more fully, individuals focus on developing unconditional love and acceptance, and on not harming others. As with soul ages, people at a higher level of consciousness can get caught up in negativity and slip down to a lower level of consciousness and functioning. With soul ages, the descent is from one lifetime to the next, whereas with levels of consciousness, we can feel wonderful and be at a high level of consciousness one day, and much lower the next.

Although old souls carry a great deal of guilt and shame, they can gradually go quite high up the consciousness scale as they develop. As we go up the soul age scale, souls have more and more potential to evolve further up. Whereas a young soul would have difficulty going beyond 200 for example, old souls who work hard can develop quite a high level of consciousness. I've been working on my consciousness for forty years now, gradually going up, three steps forward, and two back, and sometimes speeding upward or falling down quite low. The spiritual journey works like that for most people.

Many indigos that I see were born and continue to be at a higher level of consciousness than most old souls, with no effort needed for this on their part. They have the potential of evolving at a far higher level than old souls can. In addition, they have more of a social consciousness than old souls do.

So, we can expect to see more people like Gandhi, Mandela, and Mother Teresa in the future.

Crystals fall in the range of 540 or higher, a level which relates to unconditional love. Thus far, only 0.4% of the world population ever reaches this level of consciousness, according to Hawkins' research in consciousness. Indigos that I've worked with are all over the map, because they're caught up in so many difficulties. However, as mentioned earlier, they have the capacity to resolve these issues quickly through connection with Spirit or with the use of energy psychology.

In conclusion, healing issues at the soul level is essential for indigos and other sensitive people to reach their full potential. Now, I'll discuss soul group issues and their importance.

Chapter 4
Soul Groups

In order to learn our lessons and grow, we reincarnate with members of our soul group over many lifetimes, until we arrive at a place of peace and harmony with all of them.

It's possible for some members of a soul group to progress beyond their group to join a new group at a higher level of evolution to work with. On the other hand, others may remain behind if they don't learn their lessons. It's even possible for a soul to go back to a much lower level of evolution. However, we generally stay together as a group for many lifetimes and help each other grow. This includes agreeing before birth to provide each other with certain challenges.

Our roles with members of our soul group change from one lifetime to another. As an example, your mother from this lifetime may have been your child, your spouse, or your best friend, in another lifetime. And in other lifetimes you may not connect with that particular soul at all.

We've spent many lifetimes with some souls that we're closely connected with during this lifetime and very few with others. As an example, you may be far more advanced than your birth family in this lifetime, and have never been connected with them before. You chose to be born in that family, with the help of our guides, to learn particular lessons.

Joshua David Stone wrote in "Soul Psychology" that each soul is part of a soul group made up of twelve soul fragments. The extended family is twelve times that – 144 members per soul group. Others believe that each soul group is made up of several hundred souls. Michael Newton, a psychologist who wrote "Journey of Souls," believes that the size of soul groups varies from four or five to more.

Soul group members share many characteristics, as do families here on earth. However, each soul is also working through their own karma and learning their own lessons. In terms of soul group members being similar, some soul groups are made up of warrior souls, others are scholarly, some groups focus primarily on the well-being of others, whereas others are very self-absorbed and mostly ignore the needs of other people. Soul group members are all of the same soul age. For example, all members of an old soul group will be old souls. All the individuals in an old soul group will be generally focused on learning and healing, unless they're caught up in survival issues. On the other hand, the individuals in indigo soul groups will all be very sensitive and more likely to be focused on the well-being of humanity.

Who we are as souls and as soul groups greatly affects the types of interactions we have with people we're closely connected with in this lifetime. What we experience with other people is also greatly impacted by the karma between us at the soul level. For example, if two souls have also been spouses many times and have also had a great deal of conflict, this will greatly impact the nature of their relationship today. The more unresolved conflict we have from past lives, the more difficult our current relationship will be. Also, the more relationships we've had together over time, the stronger the sense that we know each other and the more it can intensify everything in the relationship.

If you don't arrive at a place of peace in relation to that difficult parent, spouse, or boss, you'll reincarnate with them and attempt to resolve the difficulties yet again.

Story:

I worked with a woman who had been in conflict with her ex-husband over their children for about ten years, including fighting through lawyers and the courts on many occasions. Their two indigo children were absorbing the stress between their parents and acting it out at school. As is often the case with high-conflict couples, they blamed each other for the children's difficulties. The parents had worked extensively with a number of psychologists and mediators, among other helping professionals, with no success. Because of my ability to read difficulties at the soul and soul group levels, I saw that my client and her ex-husband were part of a soul group who were all warriors. Because of this, it was natural for them to connect with each other in this lifetime either by standing together and fighting the outside world or by fighting with each other.

She had experienced the same pattern of conflict in her family as she was growing up. When she understood this pattern in her current life as well as at the soul group level, I was able to help her resolve the patterns of conflict very easily. She had previously felt that it was legitimate for her to have a distrustful approach toward other people in her life. After gaining this new perspective and after we healed this issue at both the soul and soul group levels, she decided to revise this pattern to a more collaborative approach. She was then able to pass this learning to her children as well.

I also assisted her to send healing energy to her ex-husband. I then did some healing work within and between the members of their soul group to help resolve the conflictual energy between all of them.

As a result of this work, this couple's anger and conflict toward each other for ten years was resolved in one session. I had a few more sessions with the mother regarding her parenting of the children, as well as the children's own issues. The children were able to settle down much more as a result of this work.

I saw the mother two years later and she told me that she and her ex-husband were still at peace and cooperating regarding their children. With her new perspective and the healing we did, this client was also now able to more easily be at peace with other people as well. This continued to positively impact the children's experience with other family members and with school, as well as their peers.

I suggest that you think of the patterns in your life. If you were rejected as a child and continue to feel rejected as an adult, this is likely to be a pattern at the soul group level as well. The same applies to other types of patterns, such as abandonment, giving too much, and so on.

The same will apply for your indigo children as well, although their sensitivity and strong-mindedness result in particular types of difficulties with other people, and these are not necessarily soul group patterns.

Trying to heal those types of issues for months or even years with a therapist is working at the wrong level. You keep analyzing all your thoughts and emotions with your therapist ad infinitum, when the problem actually began at the soul and soul group levels, with the results manifesting at the personality and relationship levels. To resolve issues quickly, we must address the cause, not the just the symptoms.

As Above, So Below

Based on the multi-dimensional perspective that I use, I believe that the same issues that occur at the interpersonal level also frequently occur not only at the soul group level, but also at the cellular level.

For example, if you haven't been nurtured all your life, chances are you do not nurture yourself. Therefore, your inner child, who is in your belly, and your organs and cells are not being nurtured.

As a law of the universe states: "As above, so below." As we come to be more fully at peace and in harmony with other souls around us, we grow in capacity and harmony within ourselves, as well as at the cellular levels. Peace and harmony at all levels. The same occurs if we start with inner peace, through meditation and healing or other means, such as prayer. Then, we can spread peace into our body and among other people, as well as at the soul level. Our intention is crucial for this. We must intend to send peace at all levels – otherwise, it won't happen.

Research has shown that profound healing can be done at the cellular level, as is discussed by Joyce Hawkes in "Cell-Level Healing." Based on her training as a cellular biologist and her practice as an intuitive healer, she's determined that we can heal our issues through healing visualizations both within and between cells.

Difficulties we experience with people here on earth are usually a result of unresolved karmic issues that we carry at the soul level. Our difficulties are also related to the fact that we've developed negative attitudes toward other people - not only in this lifetime, but in past lives as well. This affects our relationships both at home and at work, and gets passed on to our sensitive kids. As extensive research on relationships has shown, the nature of our relationships has a great impact on whether we're likely to get sick as well as on how quickly we recover. The research compiled in "Awakening Intuition" by Mona Lisa Schulz explains this very clearly.

I'll give you many exercises in the next section to help you and your children heal some of the issues discussed here. This will give you greater health and peace at the cellular level, as well as greater cooperation between your physical organs, between the various aspects of your personality, and also between you and other people, including your indigo.

Because your indigo child is such a handful, he or she will stretch you beyond your capacity at times. This will either result in your getting stressed out at times, or in taking responsibility for your life and growing more fully by being more fully at peace in your heart and in your power, as well as being more sensitive to others. In essence, your indigo is pushing you to become more like an indigo yourself.

Chapter 5
Bodhisattvas:
World View, Kindness,
and
Compassion

Bodhisattva (Pronounced *boh dee sat vaa*)

Being a bodhisattva is not a soul age. It is an attitude toward life that can be taken by more advanced souls including old souls and indigos. This term comes from Mahayana Buddhism although it's a phenomenon that's common to all spiritual paths.

There are a number of paths of spiritual growth. The path of the bodhisattva is the path of service, but at a higher level. According to Patanjali's Yoga, written around 500 A.D., there are four main paths to growth:

1. The path of devotion to God, bhakti yoga;

2. The path of service, karma yoga;

3. The path of higher understanding, jnana yoga; and

4. The combination of all three, raja yoga.

The path of the bodhisattva is the path of service combined with wisdom and compassion. Wisdom in this context refers to the fact that the goal is to help others in a way that is beneficial for them, rather than a knee-jerk reaction of giving because others feel bad or because we feel guilt, without thought of whether the giving is good for them or not. For example, giving a homeless person ten dollars may be bad for them because they might use it to buy drugs. When my son was around five, six, and seven years of age, he often wanted to give homeless people a bit of money because he wanted to help alleviate their suffering. A wiser approach is to buy them a meal, or do other things for them. As one example, until recently I donated half a day on a weekly basis for two years doing healing work with a group of homeless people. The ones I worked with were sensitive people who felt they didn't deserve much. It worked really well with them. The type of healing work I do was very effective with them.

The path of the bodhisattva does not necessarily include devotion to God. Most forms of Buddhism, for example, place no focus at all on surrender or devotion to God. Others, such as Mother Teresa, Gandhi, and most saints place a very high emphasis on devotion and surrender to God. In my personal experience, the path of service and devotion with no regard to how it might benefit me has resulted in far more growth for me than any other method I've tried.

Unlike many others on the path of service, bodhisattvas are very highly focused on spiritual development in order to help others as much as possible. The goal of the bodhisattva is to help reduce the suffering of everyone rather than focus only on their own enlightenment. This is very similar to what some people call the path of Christ – focusing on selflessly giving to others. In comparison, many people on the spiritual path are focused on attaining liberation for themselves and do not put much if any energy into helping others. They help others indirectly through the energy radiating from them rather than through direct action.

Some bodhisattvas are teachers, others are healers, and some simply serve others selflessly as mothers, bakers, nurses, or farmers. Lama Surya Das gives many examples of this in his book, "Buddha Is as Buddha Does." They lovingly and selflessly do their duty with no focus on material gain. They serve other people or they serve God – the result is the same.

Some examples of more socially conscious bodhisattvas include:

1.   The Dalai Lama, who teaches everyone to be more fully at peace with themselves and the world;

2.   Mahatma Gandhi, who worked to free India from the oppression of the British;

3.   Mother Teresa, who helped to alleviate the suffering

of the "lowest of the low"; and

4. Nelson Mandela, whose efforts helped to liberate South Africa from oppression.

These are not regular advanced spiritual people. They're very powerful, as are indigos, but they are much more so than most indigos. These bodhisattvas put most of their energy toward helping to alleviate the suffering of mankind. The vast majority of bodhisattvas are not heard of in the media and are not out to transform society and destroy governments. The four included here are meant as examples of what can be done by people with strong spirit and persistence.

As I mentioned earlier, the Dalai Lama tells us that being kind and compassionate to others is for our own good. Research has shown that focusing on the well-being of others by having kind thoughts for everyone and being kind is far better for our overall health than simply focusing on our own personal world. Some of this is discussed in "Destructive Emotions," a summary of the discussion between the Dalai Lama and a group of Western scientists. The Dalai Lama's perspective is that we need to assist in relieving the suffering of everyone around us as well as that of Mother Earth, and that this is the best path to positive growth for each one of us.

From the perspective of the Bhagavad Gita, the holy book from Hinduism that is reportedly 5,000 years old, the goal is to serve and surrender to God, and to leave one's well-being in God's hands.

In the Christian path, there is also a great deal of focus on assisting the well-being of others. In fact, Christianity focuses more on the well-being of the downtrodden than any other religion does. For example, Rick Warren discussed this in "The Purpose Driven Life." Mother Teresa was a shining example of an individual who focused intensely on the suffering of the poor and the dying.

The Dalai Lama also says that the main goal is for us to serve. In "Truth vs. Falsehood," David Hawkins quotes him as saying: "It is not enough for religious people to only be involved with prayer; rather, they are morally obliged to contribute all they can to solving the world's problems." A major tenet of this philosophy is that we need to assist in helping to alleviate the suffering of all beings.

Interestingly, and very sadly, at the same time as the churches have experienced the loss of many members in their congregations, research has shown that people have been doing less and less volunteer work for all types of groups, whether affiliated with a religious organization or not. This research has been discussed in "The Cultural Creatives" by Paul Ray and Sherry Anderson. Hence, more and more people have been developing a narrower and narrower perspective, focusing on their own needs and that of their loved ones – cocooning. They've become more and more isolated and smaller in the process.

All of us can choose to be budding bodhisattvas. It's too much to expect infant, baby, and young souls to develop a generous orientation toward everyone else, but souls who are at the mature level or older can help humanity according to their capacity – as long as they have been able to resolve blocks that interfere with their consideration for the best interests of others. Some mature souls tend to be too caught up in their own drama to give much. This also applies to some old souls who are caught up in survival issues or other major difficulties. When we're stuck in our own suffering, we can't easily have a broad perspective that includes others with kindness and generosity. Finding healing techniques that resolve the stuck blocks can release new energy that will increase our well-being as well as our ability to give. As research shows, giving to others will in turn help us to feel better and healthier.

This book includes how mature souls, old souls, indigos, crystals, and rainbows can be more fully on the path of the bodhisattvas and how we, in these interesting times, can make the best use of our gifts to help humanity evolve. Since I'm a healer, my path will be to teach interested readers and workshop participants advanced methods of healing themselves and others.

One of the results of the path of the bodhisattva is that, as we practice it more and more, we end up surrendering more and more fully. As we do so, the world then unfolds with abundance, without effort on our part. When something is needed, it simply arrives. The perspective here is that God looks after us as we are more fully in devotion and surrender. In comparison, those at a lower vibration, such as young souls, get what they need through their own efforts.

The intermediate position between those two positions relates to people who are attempting to become rich through manifesting with the law of attraction.

To be or not to be, that is one of the questions. Many of us on the spiritual path place great emphasis on beingness – being one with our spirit, being one with our partner, being one with God, being one with humanity. This involves being in our heart and spirit, but it also has to involve accepting our shadow, our dark side, more and more fully as well.

Many people do not focus on accomplishing much in the world, including alleviating the suffering of others. Their focus is on simply being. On the other hand, some people are very much into becoming and accomplishing – human doings. They're into accomplishing as much as possible, accumulating money, looking for the right partner, wanting a great career. In order to accomplish, we have to be in our power and take action in the world.

What if we combined the two into a "wholistic" approach? Not just "holistic" in the sense of going more and more toward the holy but in terms of the whole - being and accomplishing. This involves bringing together the Eastern style in terms of focus on *being* with the Western orientation toward *doing* and creating; becoming a fuller, richer human being and giving more to the world.

How does all this fit with old souls, indigos, and bodhisattvas? Well, many old souls are very much into working toward becoming better human beings and trying to be more connected with their spirit. They're also trying to resolve guilt and shame. But many aren't very grounded, practical, or accomplishing a great deal in the material world.

One of the options for old souls is to work toward the next level of being – toward being like an indigo. As we discussed earlier, indigos are very intelligent, intuitive, sensitive, and powerful. Old souls are already quite intelligent, intuitive, and sensitive, but not as much as indigos. They could build on that. The one area where old souls need the most work to become more like indigos is to develop their personal power more and more fully. Most old souls could give more to the world while they still have sizeable imperfections, rather than wait until they are more well-rounded – or wait until they're absolutely perfect, as many do. Of course, none of us will ever get there. The reality is that we're multi-dimensional beings who will get in touch with more and more facets of ourselves as we grow. The world needs our help, no matter how imperfect we are.

Indigos also could use some transformational work. Although they're very intelligent, they're not always discerning. For example, although indigos clearly express what's on their mind, it would be best for them to learn to express themselves in a way that does not turn people off. Otherwise, when people get turned off by their efforts, it becomes all too easy for indigos to shut down as well. Also, indigos may risk getting kicked out of their home or school as a result of expressing themselves repeatedly in a harsh or inappropriate manner.

Indigos also need to learn how to master the art of protecting themselves energetically as well as transforming the negativity that affects them. Remember, all negativity is actually positive. It's like manure – it's here to help us blossom more fully. They also need to learn to use their sensitivity to become more sensitive toward themselves and others – and to do this for the higher good.

Rather than use their intuition to help themselves and others, indigos sometimes say – "this is too hard," "why bother," or "you're a jerk." When indigos are off base or misdirected, they may use their power to bulldoze other people, attack themselves because of self-hatred, or lash out in the community.

Can you imagine how the world would be different if indigos integrated their gifts, maximized their abilities to help out in the world, and gave a hand to lost souls and other beings? And if old souls did the same? Wow, what a treat it would be to live here on earth!

Chapter 6
Healing Methods
for the Various Soul Ages

The strengths stemming from earlier soul ages must be balanced or integrated healthily into our present life, and weaknesses from earlier soul ages must be resolved if we wish to evolve more and more fully. How to do this is one of the challenges facing healing practitioners today.

A typical error made by most Western psychologists and counselors is that they only focus on resolving difficulties at the personality level. On the other hand, a common error made by many holistic practitioners is that they focus only on helping us to grow as souls. Instead, they ignore issues at the personality level as well as our self-destructiveness and our more primitive drives that stem from our ancestors as well as earlier soul ages.

In my view, the goal for our growth is not to try reaching for the highest level possible right away. Our goal should be to fulfill our capacity at the soul level that we're currently at and to strive to go up from there – always keeping in mind *what we can do at every step as budding bodhisattvas to help other people*.

Rather than shooting very high and ignoring our needs and the needs of others here on earth, I believe it is for our highest good to focus on clearing the luggage/karma we carry as well as focusing on the steps above us. For example, as I mentioned earlier, old souls can work toward becoming more like indigos. Old souls would do well to focus on having more of the qualities that indigos are strong in – more discernment (more intelligence and understanding), more intuition, more sensitivity (and to learn to master that rather than getting caught up in negativity), and especially, to become more powerful. Different old soul individuals will need to focus more on one or another of these elements.

Old souls can choose to follow in the path of well-balanced indigos, even though many old souls will not be interested in expending much energy helping to reduce the suffering in the world.

I believe that the main task for indigos is to learn how to heal and improve the balance or integration of the four core qualities (intelligence, sensitivity, intuition, and power) and to grow multi-dimensionally, as they work toward breaking down old structures in the world. Hopefully, they will learn how to do so without being put on medication for ADD and ADHD, or given anti-psychotic medications, thrown in jail, damage their brains on drugs, or commit suicide in the process. Regrettably, I have seen quite a number of very special individuals badly damaged by one or more of these self-destructive paths. On the other hand, there are some indigos who are in such difficulty that there's no choice but to use medication to help them stay sane and remain alive.

Indigos would do well to learn to help others and to have as much impact as possible in the world without destroying themselves in the process. A challenge that affects a great many indigos as well is that they need to learn patience and humility. They need to remember, as Confucius, the Chinese philosopher told us 2,500 years ago, that a journey of a thousand miles begins with a single step.

Indigos also need to learn how to channel their anger constructively and to live in their heart and in peace, as crystals do.

The healing methods discussed in this book are oriented especially toward old souls and indigos. However, I've experienced healing visualizations and the other methods described here to be very beneficial for infant and baby souls as well.

Mature souls can benefit most from methods that focus on forgiveness and on developing healthy relationships. Other soul ages can benefit from developing healthy relationships as well.

Young souls have no interest in healing or therapy unless they want something in particular. Young souls usually don't benefit from helping methods in general, whether traditional psychotherapy or other healing methods, unless they see it as being useful in suiting their purpose of getting more of what they want in the world.

For example, I've seen quite a few husbands over the years that were being left by their wives because the husbands had ignored their wives' concerns over the years. They rushed to my office in order to try to salvage their marriage. When the wife agreed to work on the relationship and they remained together, the men soon got back to the same old behaviors as soon as the crisis was over because the men were interested in keeping their wives for their own benefit, not in improving the situation with their wives.

If a person has trouble expressing their needs clearly with a young soul, counseling is of little value because young souls have no real interest in the well-being of the other person, including their spouse, unless it benefits them very directly and over the short-term. What's needed when old souls are in relationships with young souls or have them as bosses is to try to develop win-win agreements, set strong boundaries, set short-term goals that are reviewed regularly, and consider moving on with their lives if these are not respected.

This is different with old soul husbands who've been focused on other issues to the detriment of their relationship. These men are more likely to feel guilty sooner and take action to repair the damage. However, if the wives consider separating, these men are more likely to take action and stick with it if they still value the relationship.

Healing methods that work best for one soul age may also be of use for some of the others soul ages as well. For example, forgiveness of others is a method that is most useful for mature souls, who are caught up in the drama of relationships, but it is also beneficial for people from other soul ages. Forgiving oneself is particularly useful for old souls, who specialize in feeling a great deal of guilt, but it can also be very useful for indigos as well. Healing from shame is crucial as well, although little of value is currently available for this in the West. I've included a very powerful method for healing shame in the next section of this book. In addition, connecting with nature and with Spirit is not only useful for infant and baby souls but also for the older soul ages.

The focus of this book is that indigos will do best if they focus on serving others as best they can in a manner that fits for them. In the process, they need to open their hearts more and more, as well as be in their power, and surrender the results of their efforts to Spirit in their pursuit of reducing suffering and improving others' lot in life. Of course, as their parents, we need to practice modeling this for them. It will greatly help our own lives as well – I can assure you.

Just remember that we all get lost at times. The way the universe has been designed, we all need help from others when we get lost. Going through dark nights of the soul, when we feel completely lost and in despair, is a natural part of growth which helps us give up layers of our ego and go more and more fully into Spirit. There is no need to hide in shame when we go to those places.

When you're lost, I recommend that it's best to get inspiration from the writings of the Great Masters, such as Jesus, Buddha, and Krishna, as well as some recent writers, and to connect with very intuitive healers who have a broad range of skills to help you get unstuck.

A highly-skilled practitioner with a broad perspective and strong intuition will be able to assess at which level you are stuck and assist you resolve the issues. With my work, clients can tell in one session whether there's a great fit for them or not with the work that I do. I recommend that you should stay with a practitioner for a maximum of three sessions to determine if the healer will be able to help you substantially.

This book aims to assist old souls and indigos on their path toward helping themselves, the people around them, and the world more fully. The next section focuses on specific healing issues and methods of resolving the trauma and other difficulties. The stories and exercises are intended to support you in learning how to access clarity on the issues for yourself, begin resolving blocks to your energy levels, and grow your capacities for love, kindness, creativity, and generous contribution of your gifts to the world around you. When you understand this process for yourself you will be better able to support your indigo child or youth in a positive and constructive way.

PART II:

PROFOUND HEALING
FOR
TROUBLED INDIGOS

Chapter 1
Difficulties Facing Indigos

Labels and Medications

Because indigos are so sensitive, they can be thrown off base much more easily than the average person. The same applies to other very sensitive souls. As a result, many are prescribed medication. Physicians have been trained to eliminate symptoms so that people are able to function in the world. They have not been trained on how to help sensitive people cope by making use of their difficulties. Unless there's a major crisis that puts the person's life at risk, I recommend that seeing a physician or psychiatrist for medication should be a last stop, and that a variety of other methods be tried first.

Because many indigos are so strong-minded, they can easily be labeled as being a problem or a delinquent, or as having oppositional defiant disorder (ODD). Many are labeled as having attention deficit disorder (ADD), attention deficit and hyperactivity disorder (ADHD), or as bipolar. Some are labeled psychotic, because they say they can hear voices, or see angels or entities. Are they psychotic or do some of them see things that the rest of us are unable to see?

Recent research has shown that medications are being prescribed to children as young as four years old for such issues as attention deficit disorder. However, some of these medications have now been found to increase the risk of suicide among depressed youth. For more information on this, refer to the article from 2006 in Psychiatric News by Jim Rosack, among others.

Research in the field of "recovery," as it's been termed, has been having a very large impact on mental health policies in many jurisdictions over recent years. Although it's commonly believed by psychiatrists that people with severe mental health difficulties are unable to recover, research has shown that 80% of cases can greatly improve, and some can even fully recover.

For example, Ruth Ralph provided a report to the World Health Organization in 2000 in which she reported that 28% of people with major psychiatric difficulties such as psychosis fully recover, and 52% had what is termed "social recovery" – the ability to maintain jobs and have a productive life. This means that only 20% of people with severe psychiatric difficulties do not improve over time.

In addition, in 2004 Courtenay Harding compiled extensive research from around the world which showed that a large proportion of people do recover from severe mental health issues. This research is quoted by an official body in the field of mental health – the National Association of State Mental Health Programs, based in the United States.

As research has shown, medication does not fix or heal problems, it simply creates a different and temporary chemical balance so that patients don't have to feel their emotions, and can therefore cope better with life. Both perspectives are useful, but as with our body, we should not start with cutting out a major organ before determining if a new diet or more gentle holistic healing approach will work first. Which perspective do you choose for yourself or your child when you're in difficulties? If you feel hopeless, and act based on a belief that only extreme measures work, you will create a self-fulfilling prophecy. Unless there's a life-threatening crisis, waiting two or three months while you try alternative measures is not likely to make things worse for you or your child. Here's an example of this, from a case that I mentioned in the first section.

Story:

As an example of this, a university professor, his wife, and 13-year-old son came to see me recently to help him stop smoking marijuana. After assessing the situation and doing some healing exercises with him, I told them that he was trying to feel something by taking marijuana because he was so dulled by the anti-depressant and anti-psychotic medications he was taking. I could feel the negative energy coming off him as we did the healing work, but he couldn't because he wasn't in touch with what was going on inside of him. I knew that he would be able to heal his difficulties easily if he was able to connect with his sensations and feelings. I told his parents that I'd be happy to assist their son to help resolve his anorexia and his preference to be dead because he carried so much negative energy, if they would consider taking steps to gradually get him off his medication within three sessions. They refused, and so I told them that they would be wasting their money working with me. We cannot work toward opening up and healing, while at the same time shutting down with medications. The parents had been told by the medical system that their son would have to remain on medication for the rest of his life. They weren't prepared to even try to test that belief. The result is that this indigo will not be in touch with himself and will not learn to cope with his emotions, sensitivity, nor be in touch with his spirit.

My very strong recommendation is that you should not accept prescriptions for such issues as anxiety or depression for your indigo child or for yourself, before checking with two unrelated physicians, two holistic practitioners such as naturopaths, and two psychotherapists or healers who've worked extensively with indigos or other very sensitive souls. It is often tempting for parents to bow down to the judgments of authority, especially when pressured by the school system to get their child under control. I strongly recommend that you avoid giving your power away to authority figures, who simply want your child to sit still and be managed in the classroom. These professionals can be your advisors, but must never be your decision makers.

If you or your child is already on medication, it is still not too late to investigate other alternatives. Although you may have looked at twenty other methods, I recommend you try something new once again by experimenting with some of the methods recommended here. Although they may or may not work, you have nothing to lose. Your biggest challenge is that they may help to heal underlying trauma, but you will not feel it because of the medication. As with the 13-year-old mentioned above, you may want to consider doing healing work for a few sessions, and then have your medication reduced in strength to see how you make out. The goal then is to learn to cope with our sensitivity and heal underlying emotions and fears as they arise.

Why Indigos are so Label-Able

Why are indigos so easy to label? They take more space in life than most people do. They're simply more visible. As I mentioned earlier, part of the issue is that they're very sensitive – they're much more impacted by negative energy than most other people are.

Story:

John is 15 years old. His parents separated eight years ago. They were fighting quite a bit back then but have been at peace now for six years. John absorbed a great deal of their negative energy during the two years of fighting, before the separation and afterwards, just as we absorb secondhand smoke. He was relatively calm until adolescence, when he began acting out the

---

negativity that he had absorbed during their conflict. He began skipping school, arguing with his parents, getting into fights with his peers, and scratching cars with a key. He was sent to a psychologist, labeled as oppositional defiant disorder, and was treated accordingly. The underlying cause of unresolved pain from the divorce was not resolved. Being affected by the trauma of people around us is called secondary trauma.

As recent research on secondary trauma has shown, people can be very easily affected by each other's emotions, both positively and negatively, like a virus or a common cold. For more information on this, please refer to Charles Figley's book, "Compassion Fatigue: Coping with Secondary Traumatic Stress Disorder."

Story:

Susan would not tolerate any slights from anyone. When she felt attacked, she would lash out at school and get into physical fights with her peers. She had absorbed negative energy from peers bullying her over time, without being aware of what was happening. She kept blaming others for the difficulties she experienced with them, but by the time she came in to see me she was finally willing to look more closely at herself as being part of the problem. I was able to quickly help her to transform the negative energy that she carried.

Being strongly affected by others' emotions is most likely to occur in people who are sensitive and empathic. These people are sometimes referred to as "empaths." One of the factors here is that a sensitive person, such as an indigo, is more likely to be impacted by others' feelings if these people are important to them. The more sensitive the person, the more they're impacted.

Entrainment, a term used by neuropsychologists, refers to the connection between two people. This means that the brain and heart's physiological patterns become very similar in two or more people who are entrained with each other. It begins with bonding between mother and baby when the child is still in the mother's womb and continues throughout life. Women tend to be more empathic than men.

Even people who are not in touch with their emotions and sensations are also affected by these issues, although not as much as others. An example is that most people are negatively impacted by the mood of their depressed spouse. An indigo child would be far more impacted by their parent's depression, and may become depressed as well or may act it out. If you'd like to learn more research about entrainment, I recommend "Social Intelligence" by Daniel Goleman and "The Intention Experiment" by Lynne McTaggart.

Most other people can easily ignore the gradually eroding environment around them without batting an eye, and react only to changes that occur more suddenly. As an example, I went to a talk some years ago given by David Suzuki, a famous scientist and environmentalist in Canada. He said that if you put a frog in boiling water, it hops out right away.

However, if you put it in a pot of cold water and gradually bring it up to a boil, the frog will stay there until it dies. Most of us are similar to that frog. Consider how we're handling the environment and our politicians' inaction. We recycle a few cans and newspapers and believe that we've done our part. And many of us remain in jobs that are very unhealthy for us for years.

Being very sensitive and powerful, indigos aren't prepared to simply put up with very negative environments. They may not be able to verbalize what's troubling them, and they may get sick or act out rather than express their discomfort. But they will not simply remain passive and cope with the negativity, as most of the rest of us have learned to do.

As a result of reacting strongly to negativity around them, they're more likely to be labeled as unhealthy, troublesome, or dysfunctional. Parents, school counselors, psychologists, and other professionals then try to teach them to conform. If they don't, we take them to a physician or psychiatrist who will usually put the child on meds. What we are in fact doing is breaking the child's spirit. Horses won't perform as well as they could if we break their spirit. The same applies to our children.

Although most of us have learned to obey our elders, we now need to assess when to teach our children to do the same, and when to let them take a stand and say "no" to what they experience as being unhealthy. And they may not agree with our views. We need to talk it through with them, once they're old enough, and help them understand our perspective as we need to understand theirs.

Indigos taking a stand against unhealthy things will certainly get them in trouble with authorities sometimes, but they're here in part to help to make the world a better place.

Most of us could learn from our indigos to say "no" to people who treat us badly, to bosses who expect too much from us, to corporations that are unethical, and to politicians who say they'll protect the environment but do nothing about it. As with our indigos, we need to choose our own priorities, but looking after our eroding Mother Nature is certainly an essential one.

Part of our role as parents and other caring adults is to help indigos choose battles that are really important to them, and we can assist them with some of their issues in the process. Behind every child who has a positive impact in helping to make the world a better place is a supportive parent.

Youth Who Get in Trouble

When they're off base, indigos tend to act out or withdraw more intensely than other youth. Here are a few examples.

Some of them withdraw very deeply. I've had a couple of clients who were practically catatonic – almost like statues. One was a 28-year-old male, who didn't say two words during the entire session. Another, also male, was sent to a number of psychiatric institutes for treatment because he was so withdrawn. He spoke very little to anyone. Both had been vaccinated at clinics and at school when they were young in order to protect them from illnesses. Both mothers, who didn't know each other, were convinced that their children's difficulties began right after their children were vaccinated.

I've worked with a number of young people over time who were sent to psychiatric hospitals for treatment. Many did not benefit from that and some actually became worse because they absorbed negative energy from the other patients.

Other indigos sit on the couch and do nothing productive. They avoid life. They play video games or read comics, day in and day out. They don't engage in any useful purpose and refuse to be active participants in their own lives. In my experience, far more indigo youth and young adults have this type of problem than the other types mentioned here. They've gone on strike. They've given up on life because it all seems so irrelevant and pointless. Some give up at a very young age, sometimes as soon as they're born. Partly because of their refusal to take responsibility for their lives, they're likely to end up in trouble at school, unless they're quiet.

Story:

Toni is in grade seven. She refuses to go back to school, be home schooled, or take on any other responsibilities. Her parents make entreaties and threats, but she just sits there. It's clear that either some of her needs are not being met or she carries some kind of negative energy, but her parents have no idea what to do or how to get the situation assessed accurately. They continue with

---

their begging and threatening, which only makes things worse.

I'll discuss this and other parenting issues briefly near the end of this book, and in more detail in a future book on parenting indigos.

I've also worked with many indigos who've graduated from high school but refused to go on to further education or to work.

Story:

Mark's parents make threats regarding his being glued to the couch and not prepared to get a job or go back to school. He's now 25 and has been sitting around for several years. He goes out once in a while and takes drugs with friends a few times a week. His parents have tried nagging, pleading, and pushing, but these methods don't work with Mark. They're not prepared to practice tough love and ask their son to either work with a healer, take steps to get his life in order, or leave home because they're worried about what might happen to him if he ends up on the streets. Their fear gives Mark complete power and control over his parents, and he continues to vegetate, to everyone's detriment.

Youth such as Mark tend not to get in trouble with the authorities. Youth who lash out toward themselves or others – at home, at school, or in the community are another matter.

Tragic youth suicide. Gang violence toward an adult who was simply walking to the grocery store. At the extreme, some of these young people obtain guns and shoot other youth at school. Such shooting sprees happened less often twenty years ago, before many indigos had entered adolescence.

Many of those who withdraw or act out aggressively are not very sensitive and powerful. But, a great many are indigos.

The traditional helping system does not understand how to help many of these youth. Their reaction, after various attempts fail, is to attempt to control them. For example, they say: "You're in detention," or "You have to take medications if you want to remain in school."

In many cases, difficult indigo children have to leave school. This is particularly interesting because most school systems in North America have fewer and fewer students and their budgets are being cut as a result. Rather than learn how to help these difficult children in a way that's effective, most continue using the same old methods that don't work. In the process, they lose many indigos and other children with a variety of special needs and special gifts.

Please understand that there are some teachers and other professionals who are absolutely wonderful with indigos. It's very important for parents to try to have such teachers and professionals on their team to help their child as much as possible over time.

When parents can no longer care for their child because they're exhausted from dealing with their child and need a break, this is an opportunity for the extended family and friends to really help out, by taking in the child for a period of time or helping the child to find other living arrangements. Before it goes this far, friends and family can be a support to the parents by helping them to vent and bounce ideas around on how to handle the situation, as well as to provide breaks to the parents by looking after the child for a few hours or an overnight. In Africa, there's a saying that it takes a village to raise a child. This is even truer with indigos.

The child protection system is involved with many youth who are in major conflict at home, or have been kicked out of their home, or just choose to leave. I know this from the ten years I spent working as a family therapist with teens and their families who were involved with the child protection system. Extended family and friends can do a great deal to help in those cases. If you're an exhausted parent or have a child in difficulty, I strongly recommend that you reach out to your extended network of friends and family for support.

I will briefly discuss the context that exists regarding the difficulties of indigos and other sensitive souls before we go on to discuss specific issues and how to resolve them.

Research on our Children's Well-Being

Almost all parents want the best for their child. The only exceptions are some parents who are very neglectful or abusive to their child. However, in my experience working with them, most of those also care deeply for their child but are acting out their own pain. Unfortunately, the child protection system often tends to focus mostly on protection while ignoring the healing aspects that are needed, as a way of reducing costs. However, the result is that there are far more children in care, which greatly increases their costs. I did five years of research on the effectiveness of our work with families involved with the child protective system, and we had as good a success rate as any other program in North America, although it was less intrusive and less expensive than the other models that were available at the time.

As for less difficult situations, all of us parents can get so caught up in day-to-day living and responsibilities that we can do some things that are harmful to our child without intending to. We simply haven't taken the time to think about it or we're too busy or tired to correct the situation.

In many families these last few decades both parents are working and often the easiest solution is for busy and tired parents to leave their child in front of the TV or computer for hours at a time and/or to have them medicated if they're disruptive. The difficulties are even greater for single-parent families.

One of the issues is that many children, and especially very sensitive ones, are suffering as a result of ever-increasing pollution. More and more children have allergies and a variety of difficulties such as ADD.

A British study led by Catherine Law studying 12,500 children recently found that five-year-olds whose mothers were working watched more television, were less active, and ate more junk food than other children.

Similarly, a Canadian study published in 2009 by Mark Tremblay found that 87% of children and youth in Canada don't exercise enough and spend too much time watching TV or playing electronic devices.

Marco Di Buono of the Heart and Stroke Foundation in Canada reported very similar findings in 2009. Their findings were that 25% of Canadian children are now overweight or obese, as a result of which many will have illnesses that would not occur if they led healthy lifestyles. The result is that many will die younger than they otherwise would. In the United States, the rate is about 30% for Caucasians and nearly 10% higher for Hispanics and African-Americans, according to the American Heart Association.

A study by Paul Vengelers, connected to Harvard University, found that overweight youth are more likely to be unhappy, which could lead to unhealthy and potentially dangerous behaviors. This issue of children and youth who lead unhealthy lifestyles has become a very broad social trend.

Other research has found that when parents are stressed, their children become more withdrawn, depressed, anxious, or act out. Research reported by Carrion in 2007 has shown that the brains of children who are highly stressed because of post-traumatic stress disorder do not develop as well as other children's brains.

Recent research conducted by Saserta has found that not only do parents get sicker due to high stress, but their children are more likely to get sick as well because of the impact of their parents' stress on them.

McGowan and others have found that the DNA of children who experience abuse from their parents is permanently impacted and functions less well than that of other children. This results in their being able to cope with stress less effectively. However, as you will see below, energy psychotherapy and other methods can assist in healing those types of difficulties.

Stressed children are more likely to perform poorly in school and are more likely to have trouble in other areas as well. A part of the mid-brain called the hippocampus, whose function it is to regulate stress, is smaller in highly-stressed children. This will result in their having more difficulty handling stress as adults. This creates a vicious cycle because cortisol, a brain chemical related to stress, further damages the hippocampus, which further erodes the child's ability to handle stress. These children may be more likely to come from homes in which the parents separated when the child was small, or there is violence, sexual abuse, or neglect in the home. DeBellis and others have discussed some of the research on these issues in recent years.

Extensive research has also shown that our children suffer a great deal when their parents have mood disorders, such as anxiety or depression. Rather than deal with what's not working in our lives, many of us take a pill to suppress our symptoms. However, our children can feel it when our lives work poorly.

Twenty percent of youth do not have jobs and far more are under-employed in the U.S. As a result, many get in trouble or into drugs because they're simply sitting around being bored.

This research shows that there's a strong connection between parents' well-being and our children's. Although it would be inappropriate to think that an unwell child is always the direct result of an unwell parent, there's certainly enough research out there to prove that parents need to take steps to ensure that they are functioning at a high level and leading the kind of balanced life that includes their taking into greater consideration their children's needs, particularly when their child is doing so poorly.

Of course, we also know that such factors as pollution, being bullied at school, and living in a high-crime area can also greatly impact a child's well-being. As an example of these issues, Frederica Pereira conducted a study in New York City in 2009 that showed that children exposed to high rates of pollution have lower intelligence levels, which negatively affects them at school and in other areas of their lives.

Indigos, being more sensitive than other people, are more likely to be deeply affected by all these factors than other children because they're so sensitive. Parents, myself included, and other caring adults need to put more emphasis on addressing the risk factors affecting our children, instead of simply plugging away trying to make ends meet.

I'm not telling you all of this to make you feel bad, but to give you a wake-up call that most of us need to develop a healthier and more balanced lifestyle for ourselves and our children. Part of the difficulty is that the changes have occurred gradually, as with the frog in water gradually going to a boil. The negative reactions of so many children, including indigos and many others, are telling us that we need to do a life review now, as individuals, families, and as a society – and create healthier priorities.

When my son was having serious difficulties, we as parents decided that this had to be our highest priority. Among other things, we ended up moving to a much smaller city because of the impact of pollution on not only our son, but on the whole family. We also greatly downsized our material life. For example, I no longer have a car although I had one for decades, and I no longer have cable TV or a cell phone. In addition, I went on a two-week trip this year to California with my son, and we travelled by plane, train, and bus. We agreed that we wouldn't rent a car for even one day. I'm still looking for ways of leaving a smaller footprint on earth and developing a healthier, simpler lifestyle. We're all learning on this bus and we need to speak out with each other when we behave inappropriately, just as our indigo children are prepared to do. We all have much to learn, and we all tend to forget the essentials that we already know, especially when we're stressed.

My goal in this book is not to help you do a life review. However, if your child is off-balance, you might choose to review your income and decide how much money you'd lose if you worked a day or half-day less per week or every two weeks. Or move to a job that allows you more flex time to spend with your children. Or go for retraining to earn more with fewer work hours. Or develop a spiritual practice such as yoga or meditation, or become more involved with your spiritual community, to help you be calmer and more present. There's a great deal of research that shows that people regularly involved with a spiritual community generally live healthier lives. There are many options available to us.

Chapter 2
Becoming an Aware Participant in Healing

Now that we've set the context regarding indigos and other sensitive souls, let's get down to doing some healing work to assist you and your child to reach your potential. As discussed earlier, many issues can interfere with our well-being, including our physical health, the environment, our mind, emotions, body, relationships, and issues at the soul level. This also includes historical trauma from our ancestors. I'll show you how to do healing work regarding all of those issues. Let's now focus on a variety of specific difficulties and how to heal them.

I strongly recommend that you try the exercises for yourself before introducing them to your child. This will increase your understanding of the healing techniques and strengthen the support you can offer them. Also, doing this work for yourself will help you to be more fully at peace, in integrity, and in your personal power. This will help you in gaining further respect from your indigo, along with the benefit of having a richer life overall. You and your child will then be able to contribute more to the world.

These techniques are also for other sensitive souls, whether you have children or not. Some of you may also be adult indigos. If you're interested in exploring the topic of indigo adults further, I recommend "Indigo Adults" by Kabir Jaffe and Ritama Davidson.

Most of you will find the exercises provided here life-transforming. If you won't do the work for your own sake, I recommend you at least try them on yourself for the sake of your child. Your indigo will be able to grow and accomplish much more if you're there in the trenches with them, assisting them to heal.

As I mentioned earlier, the types of youth I've been involved with since 1969 have definitely changed. However, before I learned the term "indigo child," I worked with many young people who were very intelligent, sensitive, intuitive, or powerful. Some even had two or three of those characteristics. I began seeing more and more with all four characteristics in the mid-1990s.

In the next chapters, I'll discuss some of the main difficulties I've encountered over time in working with indigos and their families. I'll discuss approaches to healing, and include my perspective on the types of mistakes that many professionals make in trying to assist these youth and their families. I'll offer recommendations and exercises regarding how indigos and other sensitive souls can heal those difficulties. We'll focus on three main areas:

1. Internalized difficulties, such as anxiety and depression;

2. Externalized issues, such as youth who act out in the world; and

3. Negativity that comes from sources outside the child and how to help to heal those issues.

Approaches to Healing

Parents of indigo children and other sensitive souls will find it helpful to have an understanding of some of the different approaches to healing before exploring specific issues and trying the exercises to resolve them. Below is a discussion regarding what types of healing approaches are effective in dealing with various types of difficulties.

Extensive research has shown over the decades that psychotherapy and counseling overall have an effectiveness rate of about 72%. The field defines effectiveness as at least 50% of a client's concerns being resolved, or the concerns are resolved at least moderately. This includes a combination of all methods of counseling and psychotherapy with all levels of experience and training on the part of practitioners. However, some methods are more effective with certain issues, and some qualities or practitioners increase the rate of effectiveness as well.

I'll now give you a quick summary of some of the main models in the field of psychotherapy, using self-hatred as an example of an issue for discussion purposes. Using myself as an example, because of the degree of shame and self-hatred I experienced when I was younger, going to psychiatrists and psychologists who used traditional Western approaches was not helpful to me.

The Various Therapy Models

From Freud's point of view, part of the superego, the conscience, is too powerful, resulting in the patient's being very self-critical. This can lead to self-hatred. The goal of the analyst is to work with a patient on an ongoing basis so that the patient can have a corrective emotional experience through the relationship with the analyst, as well as a better understanding of the causes of his difficulties. Freud's ideas were useful to help me understand the unconscious, but they didn't help me feel any better.

My impression is that Freud's approach and other psychodynamic methods work quite poorly for most people who've experienced such issues as sexual abuse, neglect or violence, or who are adult children of alcoholics. This perspective is supported by the summary of the extensive research on depression discussed in Gerrig and Zimbardo's review of psychology in 2008. It shows that psychodynamic therapy is only 6% more effective than if clients only used a placebo – a pill containing sugar, but believed to be the real thing.

Classical psychoanalysis, developed by Freud, is rarely used now because it's very expensive, takes a long time, and is not considered very helpful by most practitioners.

However, the concepts of resistance and defense mechanisms are still useful to consider. You can relate this to when you or your indigo go into denial or rationalize, or when you repress unwanted thoughts or emotions. Projection refers to when we put our feelings onto someone else, such as saying someone is angry or untrustworthy when it actually refers to us. Regression is another type of defense, when we act as though we were younger when we go into a state of high anxiety. These coping mechanisms actually prevent us from growing. We need to see ourselves clearly, own our ways of coping that are not helpful, and let them go. We will discuss these issues in more detail at the end of this section beginning on page 278.

With supportive methods, such as Rogerian therapy, the therapist or counselor is supposed to show non-judgmental acceptance of the client, be genuine and empathic, and have unconditional positive regard. The goal is to help the client's self-esteem improve. This method tends to be most helpful for people whose mental health is fairly good. However, as research has shown, therapists who demonstrate Rogerian qualities of being genuine, empathic, and having unconditional positive regard for their client are more effective, regardless of which model they use.

In the same way, for you to help yourself, it's important to be kind and non-judgmental toward yourself. Judging yourself harshly when you discover your unresolved issues only makes things worse. In order to heal, you need to be prepared to accept yourself unconditionally while exploring what the issues are.

Solution-focused therapy is a very useful method overall, and is particularly helpful for people who have a low level of trust in helping professionals. With this model, the practitioner helps to build on the client's strengths and resources, rather than focusing on the client's difficulties.

With the solution-focused approach, the therapist focuses not on the problem but on what is happening when the problem is not occurring. You can use this on yourself or your child by asking the following questions, assuming your child is old enough to answer these questions:

- What where you doing when the situation was a bit better?

- Tell me about when this happened most recently.

- What were you doing differently at those times?

- You then ask the person to do more of what they were doing when the problem was not happening.

If we're unable to think of exceptions when the problem is absent, then the goal is to just experiment and do something different and see what happens. This model helps clients feel better about themselves and reduces resistance to moving forward.

This method has been found to be highly effective with any type of mental, emotional, and behavioral difficulty, including addictions. Also, research has shown that difficulties can be resolved in an average of three sessions. This is much quicker than most other approaches. However, solution-focused therapy is effective in only 60% of cases, as compared with an average of 72% for counseling in general, although the latter usually take far more sessions to resolve.

However, other methods are needed to assist those who don't benefit from the methods discussed thus far and who want to actually heal the causes of their difficulty. I recommend you consider using the solution-focused approach with indigos, particularly when they're very stuck and digging in their heels. This method can work particularly well to help them access their strengths, rather than try to help them see reason, because they're so strong in terms of self-referencing – relying on their own perspective, their own truth, not on another's perceptions.

Another approach used by many therapists and psychologists is behavior therapy, or cognitive behavior therapy. Cognitive behavior therapy has a good success rate, but the pace of resolution and growth is quite slow. It's not uncommon for clients using this modality to work with a therapist for 12 to 18 sessions for change to occur regarding such issues as anxiety.

One of the valuable outcomes of these models is a chart that's used by many child treatment centers. The goal is to focus on success rather than punishment.

You can create the chart as follows:

1. List desirable behaviors that you would like your child to learn;

2. List undesirable behaviors that your child exhibits;

3. Make a list of privileges that your child can

acquire through an accumulation of stars or points through increased positive behaviors and decreased undesirable behaviors;

4. Assign values to the chips or stars, i.e., five stars are required for the privilege of watching one hour of television; and

5. Be consistent with the system for at least four weeks.

It's best, if at all possible, to arrive at an agreement regarding these issues with your child. For more information on this and related methods, check Alan Kazdin's book on parenting defiant children.

Similarly, family therapy has been proven to be very effective with many troubled youth. The focus is to improve such methods as communication, parenting skills, connection between parent and child, and resolving the symptoms. I'll discuss family issues in detail in a future book on indigos and their families.

The family therapy models that have been extensively researched and found to be most effective regarding families with a delinquent, and/or other difficult issues, are outlined below.

Functional family therapy by Sexton and Alexander focuses primarily on improving communication between parents and teens, as well as on behavior change. It includes a focus on reducing negativity and blaming in the family, increasing positive communication, improving communication with the school, and so on.

Multisystemic therapy by Hengeller and others focuses on resolving such issues as low parental monitoring of their child's activity, low affection, and high conflict, all of which have been found to result in a higher rate of delinquency in youth.

Multidimensional family therapy by Liddle and others helps to resolve parenting styles that are more likely to result in youth's substance abuse, parenting styles that focus on influence rather than control, as well as assisting the youth to develop a variety of skills that are age appropriate for them.

Brief strategic family therapy by Szapocznik and others builds on models called structural family therapy developed by Minuchin, and problem-solving therapy developed by Haley and Madanes. The goal is to resolve symptoms by changing interactions in the present.

Although far less extensively researched than the above models, I've also developed a method of family therapy with clients involved with the child protection system, including a focus on parent-teen conflict, substance abuse, and so on. Our research found it to be as effective as any other in North America at the time, and more cost-effective. We experienced an 86% success rate over an average of about eight one and a half hour sessions per family. However, this research was not peer reviewed or published. This did not include the healing work described in this book, so our success rate could be expected to be higher at this point.

When governments could afford it, they paid for therapists and counselors to work with clients who had experienced such difficulties as family violence and sexual abuse for years, even though these approaches were often moderately helpful at best. Now, efficiency is very important in most programs, although many programs hire counselors with relatively little training in order to pay them less. The result is that their effectiveness will generally be lower unless they receive extensive training regarding the clientele they're working with.

Holistic Healing Approaches

Many people have turned away from such traditional helping professionals as psychologists and counselors because they believe that traditional approaches aren't very helpful. Part of the issue is that many helping professionals don't have holistic perspectives or practices to make their work more effective. As a result, many people go to holistic practitioners, most of whom have little or no training to address such issues as substance abuse, family violence, parent-teen conflict, and troubled youth.

This is part of the broader trend of more and more people moving away from the patriarchal and traditional toward a more holistic perspective – from traditional religion to a broader spiritual view, from physicians to naturopaths and other holistic healers, from medication to herbs and other natural forms of treatment, from traditional school systems to alternative approaches and home schooling.

I'm not aware of research that has credibly evaluated holistic models in treating such populations as troubled youth. We can guess that it might be about the same success rate as when traditional methods are applied.

I strongly believe that professionals are needed who are well-trained in both worlds, i.e., traditional Western methods of individual and family therapy, and in more holistic methods that take mind, emotions, body, spirit, and relationships into consideration. The goal is not to replace traditional methods with holistic methods, but to use methods that fit the situation, using a combination of traditional and holistic approaches as needed in each particular situation.

When working holistically, I've learned to use a variety of energy healing methods for different purposes. I'll discuss some of these in the following sections. As an example of a method that works very well with some issues and not others, many people have learned to visualize white light to help them to heal difficulties. That tends to work quite well, although I've learned from experience that it's not powerful enough to heal more difficult issues, such as shame.

The more precise your aim is, the more you can hit your target. If you put your energy into healing shame in general, it will result in some benefit. However, you'll be far more effective if your goal is very specific and you focus on healing the exact causes, such as with what makes you nervous about public speaking.

When I speak of visualization, it's not necessary for you to be able to see the energy. As research has shown, it's the intention that's crucial. You also need to use awareness.

For example, you intend to send energy to your belly and imagine it healing the negativity there, and moving the negative energy out through the soles of your feet. Maintain your awareness while you're doing that. There's a great deal of research that has focused on the power of intention. Readers who are interested in this research may want to read "The Intention Experiment" by Lynne McTaggart.

Although the research on the effectiveness of energy psychology is limited because this field is so new, it's been shown to be very effective in helping to heal trauma and other difficulties. It's far more effective in healing trauma than traditional Western modes of healing.

The most extensively used research model in treating these types of difficulties is EMDR – Eye Movement Desensitization and Reprocessing. For more information, check the reference at the end of this book under Francine Shapiro. Although this model is not always thought of as fitting under the umbrella of energy psychology, I believe that EMDR is sufficiently similar in its method and results to warrant being included.

Extensive research has shown that EMDR is much more effective and efficient than most other methods for healing trauma. For more info about EMDR, you can refer to such books as "EMDR: The Breakthrough Therapy" by Francine Shapiro or "EMDR Essentials" by Barb Maiberger.

In their book titled "The Promise of Energy Psychology," David Feinstein and others discuss a brain scan in which the difficulties of a client with severe anxiety are fully resolved using EFT, Emotional Freedom Technique, one of the methods of energy psychology. Feinstein has also written an article discussing the effectiveness of resolving war trauma, which was very impressive. You can get a free copy of the manual written by Gary Craig at www.emofree.com. You can also find extensive research on this model on that website.

In addition, Daniel Siegel in "The Mindful Brain" discusses the fact that mindfulness meditation can be very powerful in helping to calm the mind. A number of therapists have now begun incorporating that approach into their practice.

These and other methods form some of the foundation of the recommendations that I provide for you in this book. As you'll see, WHEE, Whole Health Easily and Effectively, also known as the butterfly hug, is one of the foundation pieces that I recommend for resolving perceptual and emotional difficulties, along with healing visualizations. It's a combination of EFT and EMDR and just as powerful as these methods, but is simpler to use.

In the rest of this section, I'll discuss a variety of types of difficulties, and methods I've found to be very effective in treating them. I'll use in part the typology developed by DSM-IV, the handbook on personal difficulties developed by the American Psychiatric Association. The methods I propose have been extensively tested and refined in my practice over the years I've worked with indigos, their families, and other sensitive souls.

Following is a discussion of the various types of negativity that impact indigos and other sensitive souls. This applies to other people as well, although negativity often has a bigger and more noticeable impact on indigos and other sensitive souls. I'll discuss each of these areas and provide recommendations on how you can help to resolve them.

Working effectively to resolve difficulties needs to include a focus on:

1. The appropriate levels;

2. The appropriate unresolved energies;

3. The causes; and

4. Its impact on specific relationships, if any.

For example, you'll fail in your efforts if you're trying to help resolve a child's anxiety by focusing only on the child, while ignoring the fact that the parents are arguing every day. Instead, you need to deal with the cause by reducing the parents' conflict. And then you can help transform the negative energy that the child has picked up from the conflict between the parents. The child might also have distanced from both parents, and this needs to be resolved as well.

Another aspect of this is a child who is hyperactive. The child may be reacting to a whole host of issues, such as red dye in his diet. That needs to be dealt with directly, rather than first trying to control the child's behavior or introducing medication.

Story:

As an example, a psychologist recently referred her 17-year-old son to me to help resolve his anger. I saw him for one session and then suggested that he and his mother come in together. However, she refused to come in to explore the possibility that she might be part of the problem, or even part of the solution. Part of his difficulty was his parents' separation when he was small. She could have assisted to heal this very easily if she had been more open. Her reaction is in part a reflection of her clinical training. It's the perspective of many psychologists that problems are inside the person and have nothing to do with the people who interact with them. As you'll have realized by now, I believe that this is far too narrow a focus for most clients who've tried various things to heal, and with no success.

Although working at the individual level was important with this youth, I also needed to work on the current relationship between mother and son as well as on unresolved issues from the past. I would also have checked if there were issues that needed to be resolved at the soul level. This work does not need to take long even though work is done at a variety of levels. Two or three sessions would have been enough.

This is an example of the fact that what prevents change is generally due to our attitudes, such as hopelessness or a narrow perspective, rather than being due to the degree of the difficulties or duration of the problems.

Some difficulties, such as a youth's depression, may have many causes. In some cases, you'll need to help resolve each of the difficulties that impact the child before you see much progress. To resolve the difficulties, you need to find a way to pinpoint the causes as precisely as possible. The most effective methods that I've found, which I teach in my workshops, involve the use of applied kinesiology, otherwise known as muscle testing, and the use of a pendulum. These, along with appropriate charts, give you very precise information as to the causes and how to resolve the issues very quickly.

Gender-Related Issues

Mash and Barkley, authors of a recent textbook titled "Childhood Psychopathology," state that extensive research has shown that males experience certain types of difficulties whereas females experience different types of concerns. ADHD, autism, childhood disruptive behavior disorders, and learning and communication disorders have all been found to be more common in boys than in girls. On the other hand, most anxiety disorders, adolescent depression, and eating disorders have been found to be more common in girls.

Preschool boys and girls are more similar in terms of the types of difficulties they experience. Across cultures, boys have been found to display more fighting and more impulsiveness than girls. Difficulties in females are more common beginning in adolescence and throughout adulthood.

Conduct disorders and hyperactivity have been found to be more common in 12- to 16-year-old boys than in girls, whereas emotional problems have been found to be more frequent for girls than for boys in this age group. In addition, research by Tolan and Foa has shown that females are more likely to be affected by trauma than males.

The next chapters will focus on how to help resolve internalized difficulties. Internalized difficulties refer to concerns that are experienced inwardly, such as shame, self-hatred, grief, depression, feeling alone or unwanted, guilt, anxiety, anger, rage, fear, and trauma.

Later chapters will focus on externalized difficulties. These refer to the difficulties that have an impact in the external world, such as acting out toward persons or objects. The last chapter in this section focuses on causes of difficulties that stem from outside the child.

SECTION I:

INTERNALIZED DIFFICULTIES

Internalized Difficulties

As I mentioned on the previous page, internalized difficulties refer to issues that are experienced inwardly, such as anxiety, depression, and shame.

An essential issue regarding healing is that we're unable to heal a particular state when we're struggling inside of it. Unfortunately, many helping professionals try to help their clients that way. For example, if a client has low self-esteem, depression, or a troubled relationship, many professionals put a great deal of time and effort into helping the client to analyze the problem and its apparent causes, and helping the client to develop new beliefs and coping skills. The client may then be assisted to discuss the issues with the people involved, such as their child, their spouse, or their boss. This approach, although useful in some cases, is often insufficient. The goal of this book is to address the healing aspects, not the traditional Western approaches such as cognitive therapy, communication, and so on. If the healing approaches discussed in this book don't work for you, I recommend you broaden your focus and consider using these traditional approaches, or others. In some cases, you will need to use both healing and more traditional approaches at the same time.

Chapter 3
The Essence of Transformation

In summary, my view of the essence of transformational work is that we're already enlightened beings. We already have Christ Consciousness, Krishna Consciousness, Buddha Nature, or whatever term you want to use. We're not fallen angels, but beings who simply need to remember who we are.

The essence of the path, in my view, is just as the Zen Buddhists have said: We're like a mirror that we need to keep cleaning when dust falls on it in order for the light to shine. To start with, there's a great deal of dust, and we need to do a spring cleaning, so to speak. And it gradually gets better and better once we've figured out how to remove the main obstructions. It then gets easier when we've dealt with the main issues – until the universe decides that it's time for our next big challenge. Our intention and our will are the crucial elements here.

Using myself as an example, I check on my energy field every morning to see if there's any dust blocking my light. I check at all levels – physical, mental, emotional, energy field, relationships, and my work. This work is multi-dimensional, because the obstructions could come from anywhere – physical illness, past life issue coming to the surface, conflict with a loved one, psychic attack, etc.

The past is gone and the future has not arrived. We need to take them into consideration, but the central focus is on how we are within our world at this moment. And the next step is how we are in the world as we take steps to help ease suffering in others.

The essence of transformation, in my view, is as follows:

- Give ourselves and everyone else around us unconditional love as best we can.

- Gain a broader perspective of our suffering. The higher perspective here is that, whenever we or a family member is suffering, we take full responsibility for it and ask, "Why is this in my life – what do I need to learn for my higher good?"

- See negativity as being an opportunity to work through karma, pay for old sins, or learn lessons that are important for us. As the saying goes, "For everything that has already happened, thank you. For everything yet to come, yes."

- When we're stuck and not making progress, it's very useful to see it as energy that needs to be transformed, rather than looking at it or the other

person as needing to be controlled or supressed,
or as pathological and needing to be medicated.

- Think of energy as flow. If we have pain in our
  heart or in our arm, if our child is suffering, or if
  we have a difficult relationship, send energy from
  above through our heart center and into the area of
  difficulty, thus helping to transform the obstructions.

- Ask for guidance from our higher self, higher
  power, or Spirit, however we define it. For heart-
  centered people, I strongly recommend that you
  consider devotion to Spirit through prayer, chanting,
  or other means.

- Surrender our petty reactions, our ego, to Spirit so
  that we may function at a higher level. It's very
  useful to see all obstructions as an opportunity to
  simplify, to surrender, and to resolve attachments
  to things we want, and wanting to avoid what we
  dislike. Just accept what is at a profound level,
  while serving. And resolve what you have power to
  change.

- Heal our issues as discussed in this book or through
  other means we've learned from other sources.

- Give ourselves and everyone else forgiveness and
  compassion for our imperfections.

- Do service work to help reduce suffering and to
  help others function at a higher level.

- Our perspective, our intention, and our will are
  crucial in our transformation.

In this context, it's useful to remember the serenity prayer from Alcoholics Anonymous:

"God, grant me the serenity to accept the things I cannot change, the courage to change the things I can, and the wisdom to know the difference."

The Methods

The following are the essential methods that I recommend for you to focus on. The rest of this section will give you methods that include these and others that are more tailored to specific difficulties. Remember, with each issue you heal, it's an opportunity to surrender layers of your ego, and attachments as well.

1) Butterfly Hug: This simple method stems from a combination of EMDR and EFT, two very effective methods for healing trauma. These and related methods have been used in many parts of the world to help people heal from trauma and other difficulties.

Focus on a particular fear, trauma, or other negative emotion that you have. The original method recommends that you cross your arms in front of your chest and rest your hands on your shoulders. Go back and forth from one hand to the other, tapping a few times each side. Keep tapping while you say three or four times: "Even though I have this …. (insert your fear or trauma), I deeply and completely accept myself and God loves me unconditionally." (Only say the latter part if you believe in God. The exercise will work whether you say that part or not.) Rather than tapping on your shoulders, I recommend that you tap your index finger and thumb together, back and forth from one hand to the other. You can make this so subtle that you can do it in the middle of a crowd, with a bit of practice, with no one knowing that you're doing healing work.

2) Ho'oponopono: A healing exercise on forgiveness from ancient Hawaii. Focus on the harm you've done others, others have done you, or harm you see in the world. Ask the Creator for forgiveness in the following way: "I'm really sorry. Please forgive me. I love you. Thank you." Say it over and over, at least eight times. I do it regularly on my prayer beads, which has 108 beads.

3) Healing Visualizations: This is a very effective approach to help heal mind, emotions, body, and spirit. There are many types for different purposes. Here are a few of the ones I find most useful.

   a) Connect with Your Spirit: Have light go in from above through the crown of your head and fill up at your heart, as well as at your mind, emotions, and body. Have nurturing and healing energy, such as Goddess energy, come into the cellular level.

   b) Try this one to heal shame, which we all carry too much of: Focus on something you've done or failed to do that still causes you shame and limits your capacity. Imagine that you have a violet flame going in through the crown of your head. Have this light go around your body and burn away the shame that binds you. Similarly, have light go to other parts of you that carry pain and suffering. It doesn't matter if you can't visualize the energy. It's your intention that counts.

c) Protection: People who are very sensitive can be greatly impacted by energy around them – whether in traffic, crowds, noise, or a person who is depressed or angry. It's essential for sensitive people to learn how to protect themselves, such as imagining a bubble of protective energy about three feet (one meter) all around them, or imagining a layer of rose pink energy right next to their body. Do this at least once a day. Do it more frequently if you're in a difficult location or if you're in conflict with someone or being attacked energetically.

d) Grounding: For personal power and confidence, place your feet flat on the floor. Imagine a cord goes down from the base of your spine deep into the earth where it's still brown or green. Hook the cord to a big rock and then make the cord a bit tight. Imagine making the cord as big as a garden hose. This method needs to be used on a daily basis to be effective. If it feels like grounding and protection don't work for you, say to yourself: "Gentle strength, gentle strength, gentle strength…" ten to twenty times in a row and see how that feels. If you prefer this method, use it as needed.

In my experience working with these healing methods, whatever you resolve with these methods is usually healed permanently, although other angles or layers may come up later. Work with one issue at a time.

e) Multi-Dimensional Healing: You'll find
visualizations related to healing various issues
throughout this book. Multi-dimensional healing
refers to healing issues at a variety of levels – our
DNA, cellular level, mental, emotional, soul, soul
group, in the land around us, etc. Here's a quick
summary of some of these methods that I use regularly:

- Have light go into your DNA to heal negativity
  from your ancestors;

- Have the light go to your ancestors to heal their
  DNA and Spirit;

- Have light go the first six inches (15 centimeters)
  over your head to clear away other people's anger;

- Have violet flame or emerald green go into your
  aura three feet (one meter) around your body to burn
  away negativity from other people;

- Have light go two feet over your head, to clear away
  negative thought forms;

- Have light go to the stratosphere to clear away
  negative thinking from humanity's collective
  unconscious that negatively impacts you and other
  people;

- Have nurturing and healing Goddess energy go to
  your belly to nurture your inner child;

- Have Spirit go to your loved ones to help heal their
  wounds;

- Ask the Lords of Karma to repair your energy centers - your chakras and meridians;

- Ask Archangel Vywamus to heal and expand your energy channels – your sushuma, which is your central energy tube, along your spine, and your nadis, which are like your nervous system, but at the energetic level;

- Ask the Lords of Karma to heal the extension of your sushuma above you to be healed. This is called the galactic cord and goes all the way up to the Godhead. Ask for the same for your cord that goes all the way down to the core of the earth;

- Have light go into your heart chakra, in the center of your chest and send that to the heart chakra of a person you're concerned about. Then ask Spirit to send that person healing energy, from above to that person, specifically to the area where they're having difficulty.

- Ask Krishna and Kali to immediately transform all energies from dark to light from the Dark Side of the Universe that are attacking you, your loved ones, and other aspects of your life;

- Ask to heal your soul group and ask that your souls be unified;

- Imagine you carry wounded God or Goddess energy and ask Spirit to heal them and to unify them within your being;

- Ask to be filled up with the energy from your favorite high being – such as Christ, Krishna,

Mother Mary, Buddha, Kuan Yin, etc. Do this regularly so you become more and more like them;

• Ask Spirit to send healing energy to an area you're concerned about, such as Haiti, or an impoverished neighborhood near you.

I'll give you some examples near the end of this book of how I used some of these healing methods on my recent trip to assisting in the healing work in Haiti.

Let's now review more specific areas that need healing work.

Types of Internalized Difficulties

There are a number of types of issues that relate to internalized difficulties, which we'll discuss in this section on how to heal them. These include:

a. Trauma;

b. Secondary and vicarious trauma;

c. Historical trauma;

d. Shame;

e. Guilt;

f. Self-hatred; and

g. Suicide risk.

Trauma

Trauma is a major difficulty experienced by far more people than most of us realize. In fact, all of us carry what is termed historical trauma. There are three main types of trauma:

i) Trauma;

ii) Secondary trauma and vicarious trauma; and

iii) Historical trauma.

Chapter 4
Trauma

Trauma is normally defined as two separate issues, with a number of separate components. First, a person has experienced, witnessed, or been confronted with an event or events that involve actual or threatened death or serious injury, or a threat to the physical integrity of themselves or another. It can include a serious threat or a sudden destruction of one's environment. Second, the person's response involves intense fear, helplessness, or horror. This results in post traumatic stress disorder – PTSD.

There are three main aspects to PTSD:

- Re-experiencing the event through reminders or in dreams;

- Avoidance and/or numbing through efforts to avoid thoughts, feelings, or activities, diminished interest in significant activities, and disconnection; and

- Persistent arousal, such as difficulty falling asleep, irritability, difficulty concentrating, and hyper-vigilance (being constantly wary and afraid).

If you or a loved one have experienced some of these symptoms for some time but aren't sure why, think back to when the symptoms started and whether they followed an incident that was traumatic. However, symptoms can sometimes begin a fairly lengthy period of time after a traumatic incident.

Some have been in car accidents, for example, and the physical or emotional impact still affects them years later. As an example of this, a participant in one of my workshops had not driven a car for many years following a car accident. I was able to help her resolve the difficulty in two or three minutes using an energy psychotherapy method that I'll teach you below.

Others have been traumatized as a result of conflict between their parents during the breakdown of their marriage. Some grew up in a dysfunctional family where there was substance abuse, neglect, violence, or sexual abuse. Others were in a violent marriage and are now terrified of getting into a new relationship. I've worked with some families in which the child, sometimes an indigo, threatened to or beat up their parents or a sibling. The effect of the trauma can continue for decades as if the incident had occurred very recently. The person suffering may have tried many different methods to heal, but with little success.

A person's way of coping may also make things worse. Some withdraw from their loved ones or from favorite activities. Some go on disability from work for many months or years. Others abuse alcohol or drugs. Others take prescription drugs for years and numb all their feelings as a way of coping with their fear and anxiety.

Most forms of psychotherapy are unable to heal PTSD. A clear example of this is that more soldiers who went to Vietnam died from suicide after returning home, than soldiers who were killed in combat. Many committed suicide even though a great deal of money was spent by the U.S. government on psychiatrists and psychologists to help them. Appropriate methods of healing had simply not yet been developed.

However, new forms of trauma therapy have been developed over the past decade or two that are proving to be extremely helpful in quickly resolving these very difficult concerns. Some of these new forms of therapy are:

- EMDR (Eye Movement Desensitization and Reprocessing) developed by Francine Shapiro;

- EFT (Emotional Freedom Technique) by Gary Craig;

- The butterfly hug or WHEE (Whole Health Easily and Effectively) by Daniel Benor;

- The Tapas method (Tapas Acupressure Technique) by Tapas Fleming; and

- Somatic Experiencing, developed by Peter Levine.

All of those are well-described in the books that you'll find referenced here, although you would have to take a workshop to learn EMDR or see a practitioner who's been trained in that modality.

As I mentioned above, my favorite one, described in some detail below, is the butterfly hug, a combination of EMDR and EFT. It works wonderfully with trauma, negative beliefs, or emotions, as well as with many physical pains. The butterfly hug is simpler and easier to use than either EFT or EMDR and is just as effective.

Exercise:

Write down a trauma or a negative belief. The example below uses "I'm stupid." You write down your own negative belief and use it in the exercise.

With one hand, tap the tips of the index finger and thumb three to five times, and then do the same with your other hand. Go back and forth like this during the exercise.

Take one belief at a time and, while tapping, say the following:

"Even though I think I'm stupid because I just failed a test, I deeply and completely accept myself, (and, if it fits for you, add the following) and God loves me unconditionally."

Say this four times while tapping. Review how you feel. If it's still an issue, do the exercise again a few times. My experience is that this method helps to relieve trauma in a few minutes with about 95% of clients. However, some issues are more complex and have many aspects that need to be healed.

This method is like a laser. The more precise you are regarding the issue you want to resolve, the greater the impact of the exercise.

As another example, "Even though I'm ashamed because I just unintentionally offended that person, I deeply and completely accept myself and God loves me unconditionally." Say this four times while tapping back and forth, left and right.

Chapter 5
Secondary Trauma and Vicarious Trauma

Some of you may think the following information is a bit too weird. However, research has shown that these difficulties not only exist, but have a great impact on many people. The problem is that most of us aren't aware we carry these types of energies. It's like carrying a cold virus but not developing a cold until later. However, our indigos and other very sensitive souls feel these issues more quickly and much more intensely than other people do.

Secondary trauma, whose principal writer is Charles Figley, relates to our picking up negative energy from being around other people who are traumatized. It often relates to helping professionals. Vicarious trauma is a term that means much the same thing as secondary trauma. Compassion fatigue and emotional contagion relate to the same types of difficulties although there is some difference between the terms.

For example, a person may have compassion fatigue after looking after an aging parent for a long time or a child who has a disability that needs ongoing care, such as an indigo with ADHD who keeps getting into trouble at school. For example, if this applied to you, you would pick up and accumulate the suffering that your child experiences at school, as well as the suffering of others who complain about your child.

Emotional contagion can occur in crowds, such as in shopping centers. Some indigos and other sensitive souls find it very difficult to go into such areas because they haven't learned how to protect their energy field effectively.

One of the biggest causes of what's generally thought of as burnout is by helpers being affected by and taking on the negative energy of the people they help. Another term for this is vicarious trauma which was mentioned on the previous page. However, burnout relates to overwork, which is not the case with secondary or vicarious trauma.

The ideas in the literature on these topics are very useful, although I find methods from energy psychotherapy far more powerful for resolving burnout, compassion fatigue, and secondary and vicarious trauma than traditional Western approaches. My experience is that healing visualizations are more helpful in resolving these issues than any other method from the field of energy psychology.

Research shows that about 20% of professional helpers are greatly impacted by taking on negative energy from their clients or patients. The ones most affected tend to be more sensitive souls. The vast majority are not aware of what's happening to them because the process is very gradual. It starts with them losing their enthusiasm for their work and becoming more and more tired over time. This has serious repercussions for work performance and relationships at home as well. This applies to psychologists, child welfare workers, nurses, physicians, counselors, healers, teachers, dentists, firemen, lawyers, and anyone who deals with people under a great deal of stress.

When a parent is impacted by negativity at their work, they may not feel it themselves but they carry the negative energy in their aura. Their child, especially an indigo child or youth, picks it up and can be greatly impacted by it. They may then act out without anyone understanding the cause. Here's an example:

Story:

I worked with a 15-year-old youth whose father was a supervisor for many years in the child protection system. The youth ended up becoming more and more burdened, belligerent, and unmotivated. The major part of my work was to simply help her transform from darkness to light the negative energy that she had picked up from various places, including friends she had tried to help, but especially from the negative energy that her father brought home without his even being aware of it. In this case, the father couldn't understand what the daughter and I were talking about.

An interesting phenomenon that happens is that people who are tough and are very well protected energetically, as this father was, don't feel the negative energy at all and aren't affected by it. They bring it home and their sensitive loved ones absorb it. Their well-being or behavior is negatively impacted by this. Some wives of soldiers, police, and firemen pick up these negative energies. Indigo children are more likely to be impacted by this.

The experience of this 15-year-old happened with my son as well when he was quite young. I had my practice at home, as I still do. I discovered later that he was picking up the negative energy from my clients through me, even though I didn't feel it at the time. He then acted it out aggressively at school. As part of my growth, I've since intentionally become more and more sensitive, and can feel these energies more deeply than I used to.

Some people who are negatively impacted by these energies aren't aware of it because they're not open to feeling their own sensations and emotions. The goal for them to improve their situation is to start by becoming aware of these sensations and feelings.

Story:

A 12-year-old saw one child bully another at school. She didn't know either of them. However, she was directly impacted by the incident through secondary trauma and absorbed their negative energy. She then unknowingly took this aggressive energy home in her energy field and acted it out by bullying her mother. Once we clarified the cause of the daughter's behavior, we were able to resolve the negative energy from the incident at school in a few minutes. She then went back to her normal attitude and behavior.

Here's another example: A baby would cry because of normal needs such as hunger and needing a change of diaper. Her mother would nurture her and look after her needs. The child would continue to cry more and more. Eventually, the mother would put the baby down and the baby would stop crying. The same routine would occur frequently and the mother would pick the baby up again. The reason for the baby's crying was that the mother was carrying a great deal of traumatized energy in her field. Her baby would feel it and cry out in pain as a result. The baby cried very little when others held her.

The traumatized energy in the mother's field was there as a result of her dysfunctional childhood. Helping to resolve away the mother's negative energy from her childhood would have been very important for her baby's well-being regardless of whether the negative energy was felt by the mother or not.

As I mentioned earlier, most helping professionals trained in Western modalities don't understand these issues relating to energy. The result is that they're not able to help indigos and other sensitive souls who experience the types of difficulties discussed in this book. These professionals haven't yet developed the understanding and sensitivity, or the tools to assist in healing those issues. They also haven't learned to transform negative energy out of their own energy space. On occasion, some sensitive clients come to see me after feeling worse after seeing another practitioner who carried unresolved negative energy in their own field.

Story:

Because this issue of picking up negative energy is so crucial for you to understand, I'll give you yet another example. I had a few sessions with a very sensitive 33-year-old indigo female recently. She picked up negativity very easily from around her and then went more and more off base the more negativity she accumulated. She went into a psychiatric hospital a number of times as a result. She was labeled as bipolar, among other things. She hated herself for being so sensitive, which made things worse. Her self-hatred came in part from her experience with her father, who was very critical toward her, and told her that she always destroyed everything. She usually cried a great deal when she saw helping professionals, which triggered their need to help resolve her suffering. She was given various different medications and hospitalized. She then picked up more negative energy from the psychiatric hospital.

In each of the four sessions I worked with her, she was able to transform the negative energy that she carried very quickly with my guidance. However, she then returned to her self-critical, doubting mode and back into fear. This was a vicious cycle, which we were able to resolve more and more fully with each session.

Exercise:

Following is one of the most important exercises in this book for the simple reason that most people are not aware of the negative energy that they carry. You can use this exercise first to transform away some of the negativity that you carry, and then you can help your indigo do the same.

Imagine light coming in from above to the top of your head and focus it on your aura, the energy field about three feet (one meter) around your body. There's no effort involved in doing this. Simply intend it to happen, and it will. No need to struggle. Neurologists and mind-body workers use the phrase "Where intention goes, energy goes."

Have the light, a violet flame, go into the various layers of your energy field – the etheric, emotional, mental, and Buddhic (spiritual) layers, and burn away the negativity from your environment.

- *Etheric layer – right next to the skin, about two*

inches (five centimeters) thick;

- Emotional layer – about one foot thick, or a third of a meter, right after the etheric layer;

- Mental body – one foot thick, right after the emotional layer; and

- Buddhic layer – one foot thick, right next to the mental layer.

Burn away the various aspects of negativity from your environment that are in your aura. For example, if you live in a high crime area, burn away anger, despair, and other aspects of negativity from your community. If you're a fireman, burn away the trauma of people you've helped that lost all their life possessions in a fire. If you have neighbors who argue regularly, burn away their anger and fear from your aura.

The same applies to your indigo except that your child is likely to feel the negativity more than you do. Most of the time, neither of you will be able to identify the cause of your distress. You and your child will simply feel lighter after transforming these layers of negativity.

In addition, if you were depressed in the past, your child will need to clean up that energy from her field as well. The same applies to other types of negativity you and your spouse have gone through *since your child has been born. Use the same method to transform these from darkness to light.*

Chapter 6
Historical Trauma

Historical trauma relates to trauma that we carry at the cellular level from previous generations. Research with two different groups has shown this to be a very important issue.

The first relates to Jewish children who were in internment camps in Nazi Germany but survived the war. The research focused on their offspring who were born after the war. The research showed that the offspring experienced greater anxiety, depression, guilt, despair, and somatization than the rest of the population. Somatization refers to stress that affects one's body through illness. Felsen and Solomon also found that this group also had difficulty with relationships and attachment to others, as well as extreme reactivity to stress (refer to Levav or Tytell for more information). The second generation experienced these difficulties, even if the holocaust was never again discussed in the family.

The second group consisted of people of Japanese origin who were put in internment camps during WWII on the west coast of the United States and Canada. Their children, born after the war, experienced a reduced sense of security, heightened sense of shame, and lower self-esteem than the general population (refer to Nagata for more information).

No one is consciously aware of historical trauma because it predates us – we've always carried it. We've lived with these issues from the time of our birth and as part of our everyday experience, and they have a great impact on our well-being, including our level of stress, even if we and the helping professionals we work with aren't aware of its cause.

This type of difficulty often has a greater impact on many indigos and other sensitive souls than it does on their parents or others. It can affect them in a variety of ways, such as what appears to be ADD, physical reactions to stress, acting out, wanting to consume alcohol or drugs as youth to dull the pain, etc. I've worked with many clients who were strongly affected by this type of issue, and much more so than other family members, because of their high degree of sensitivity.

Exercise:

Think of the two world wars, the Great Depression, and other earlier events in your cultural background. African-Americans in the United States might think of their ancestors being in slavery, and those of European stock might think of multiple invasions of their countries.

Think of other possible historical trauma in your

family of origin. Break it down piece by piece. For each issue, imagine light going in through the crown of your head into the cellular level. Have the light go into the DNA in each cell and transform the old trauma from darkness to light. Feel the difference, compared with a few minutes before doing this exercise.

Teach your indigo how to do this exercise themselves, or do it for them. If they're old enough, you can discuss the experience with them.

Chapter 7
Shame

I'll discuss shame in some detail because I've found no effective and efficient technique for resolving it in either the professional or the self-help literature.

Some degree of shame is useful because it results in our behaving appropriately in public instead of following whatever impulse strikes us. This applies to guilt as well. For example, we wear clothing in public in part because of shame. Shame also restricts us from doing such things as picking our nose on the bus.

One of the aspects of shame is that most people aren't even aware of the degree to which it controls their lives. It's generally below our radar – we simply feel uncomfortable in certain situations and behave in such a way as to avoid the discomfort. Many people think of the discomfort as fear, anxiety, or depression, but the reality is that it's more often shame that binds us, preventing us from doing something that is for our highest good.

Shame shuts us down more completely than any other emotion. When we give ourselves a guilt trip, we say something like: *"I really blew it this time and hurt that person."* When we give ourselves a shaming message, it's more like: *"I'm no good," "I'm stupid,"* or *"I'm not lovable."* As you can see, guilt relates more to a specific issue, whereas shame is more generalized regarding how deficient we feel we are in our core.

Some people have guilt-ridden personalities, meaning they believe that everything's their fault. Shame, however, is an overall statement about being bad to our core. As an example, I experienced a great deal of shame and fear growing up. I must have seen over fifty helpers in an attempt to heal this, but they had no idea how to help me resolve my shame. I had to develop a new way of resolving shame, with the guidance of Spirit, which I'll share with you below.

Old souls are affected by shame and guilt more than any other soul age group, but in my experience, some indigos experience these quite intensely as well.

It's not just a negative message that impacts a child, but the energy of shame that accompanies it. People who shame children or others are passing on the shame that was put on them when they were kids. They often don't realize that they're shaming us. This carries on through the generations.

Being affected by other people's negative energy is like a cold virus. You pass it on without being aware that you even carry it. A cold makes us sniffle and sneeze. Shame diminishes us. It takes very little shaming for a sensitive indigo to be greatly impacted. This applies even more to old souls.

Shame can come from our family or from other groups we belong to, such as religion or work, and even from advertising. Think of all the girls and women who are trying to lose weight to be as super-slim as models. Shame also comes from our past lives. Let's explore these issues, beginning with our family.

Paul's dad tells him, "You're a real screw up. You can't do anything right."

This kind of message can stay with the child for the rest of his life.

As an example, I had a client who was physically abused and shamed by his father. He ended up taking it out on his wife by shaming and beating her. He was willing to look at the roots of his behavior, however, and was able to resolve these patterns very well through our healing work.

Shame also runs in some families. For instance, if a mother was sexually abused as a child and has not healed this, the negativity remains in her energy field. Her children are affected by this energy, even if they have no knowledge of their mother's abuse. Her daughter might struggle all her life with self-hatred because of a negative body image or she may be closed sexually, without being aware that she is carrying her mother's suffering.

Indigos are very sensitive to unresolved trauma from their parents' history. How about yours? Think of trauma that you experienced over the course of your life. Perhaps you were able to stuff the pain, and so it doesn't appear to have seriously affected you, but it limits you. You may feel mildly anxious or depressed. But your indigo child, being so sensitive, can be severely impacted by your trauma whether you tell him about it or not.

Shame also runs deeply in some cultures, particularly in those that have been defeated by other groups. Think of First Nations people around the world, who were scorned for honoring their so-called false gods, and seen as inferior for honoring animals and nature and not plundering the earth. In Canada, for example, many were sent to residential schools to make them like Caucasians, and many of those were also physically and sexually abused.

As a result of their experiences, many First Nations people feel that it's neither acceptable to be like the dominant culture nor their own group. They end up in a no man's land of suffering, staying as drunk or stoned as possible to dull the pain, taking out their hatred of life on their loved ones. I've seen this with many of my First Nations clients and with indigenous people from other cultures. Research summarized by Julian Burger for the United Nations has shown that First Peoples around the world have become full of self-hatred and take it out on themselves and their loved ones. We can fairly safely assume that this is also true of other groups who are oppressed.

We can also absorb shame through osmosis from watching TV, reading magazines, and so on. For example, some young women become anorexic because they became ashamed of their bodies after seeing thousands of TV commercials showing skinny models. Large numbers of women start dieting because they think they're overweight, even though this is untrue. I've read that four out of five American women are dissatisfied with the way they look. This is all about shame.

Research has shown that adults who were beaten as children were less impacted if their parents apologized and tried to make amends. The ones whose parents hit and also scorned and shamed them fared much worse. The message in these situations is: "You're worthless and you're bad, and I treat you accordingly." Of course, this was a reflection of the parents' inner state and, as we all know, no child is worthless. However, we as children internalize these messages and tend to treat ourselves accordingly.

Adult children of dysfunctional families tend to carry much more shame than people who come from healthier families. However, this does not apply to all offspring from dysfunctional families. Some developed a high degree of resilience in childhood. They learned to cope very well by turning adversity into advantage. On the other hand, many people who are very sensitive and come from healthy families also carry a great deal of shame from experiences that could be considered minor, by comparison.

Shaming not only happens at home, but can and does happen at school, at work, and in the community. Put downs and belittling are a too familiar part of childhood. A child may be put down because his ears stick out. I was put down when I went to English school because of my French Canadian background. Others are put down because of the shape of their body, because they're too tall or short or overweight, because of their skin color, or because of their family, religion, or culture.

I know of many indigos who've been shamed because they're too smart, because they dress differently or are too sensitive, because they want to do their own thing, and because they stand up to authority figures. My son was shamed at school for being too smart. He had been sharing his knowledge about science with people from the age of four, but shut all this down in grade three because other children mocked him for it.

Some refuse to go back to school because of the shaming they experienced there. Some are shamed for speaking their minds or questioning what the teacher says. Others are scorned by other kids. These issues can be very painful for children and youth. There have been reports in the news of youth committing suicide because of harassment at school, and many of those are likely to be indigos.

However, other indigos lash out toward kids who mistreat them, and they're then labeled as the problem. A recent newspaper article in my community, by Kim Pemberton, quoted research saying that the number of public school employees attacked and injured by students has more than tripled from 2006 to 2009. We can be sure that many of those are indigos, who refuse to be controlled or shamed into being quiet and just sitting. The reason for this great increase in violence in recent years, I believe, is that there are far more indigo youth now and they're less willing to submit to what they perceive as unjust as were previous generations.

Story:

Tina is part of the out crowd at school because she's wearing the "wrong" clothes. Her family simply can't afford to buy her trendy outfits. Other girls shun her and talk behind her back, making fun of her simple clothes. She reacts by withdrawing into herself, but this only makes things worse. She doesn't tell her family what's bothering her because she believes they can't help her. She becomes more and more shut down, gradually becoming depressed. She hates her life. She starts running with the wrong crowd and gets caught up in drugs.

Shame also runs in families – in some more than others. One aspect of this is when we pick up each other's energy and carry this in our energy field. For example, if a mother was sexually abused and has not healed this fully, the negativity is still in her energy field. The indigo absorbs it and as a result, may hide in shame or act out.

Kids are very adept at shaming each other. It's important to remember that even though indigos are advanced souls, they go through some of the earlier phases of soul ages, including baby and infant souls. As a result, younger souls as well as indigos may try to get others, including their parents, to conform by using shame and guilt, which is one of the core aspects of baby and infant soul ages.

Remembering that other people are simply acting out their own shame can protect us from their toxic messages. Unfortunately, we were very vulnerable as children and did not have the perspective and strength to brush off people's shaming. We are all "smaller" than we could be, largely because of shame and fear. We and our indigo children must learn to energetically protect ourselves to avoid being severely impacted by these negative energies, in part by transforming the shame picked up over time.

We also carry shame at the DNA level from our ancestors, and shame at the soul level from our own negative actions in past lives. All of these levels must be healed as we gradually ascend. I'll show you how to heal these various issues following the next quote.

As Nelson Mandela told us, quoting Marianne Williamson's book "A Return to Love," when he became president of South Africa:

"Our deepest fear is not that we are inadequate. Our deepest fear is that we are powerful beyond measure. It is our Light, not our darkness, that most frightens us."

How to Resolve Shame

Shame is more dense than most other forms of negative energy. It can't be resolved through the use of regular visualizations using clear, white, golden, or other light.

I've found little of value on how to deal with shame in the professional literature except for the writing of John Bradshaw from the field of adult children of alcoholics. In Bradshaw's book, "Homecoming," he gave a variety of exercises to heal the inner child, including how to heal shame. He also discussed it in his very aptly titled book:

"Healing the Shame that Binds You." For me personally, I found his work to be useful, but slow and arduous.

The best approach I experienced for healing shame is actually a variation of methods that stem from India and Tibet. It includes a healing visualization to transform negative energy. Their methods for visualization were borrowed a few decades ago by the athletic teams in Russia to help improve their performance at the Olympics. This proved to be very successful and visualization has gradually come to be used in many areas of life in the West now, including by a small but growing proportion of psychotherapists. Many mind/body healers also make extensive use of visualization.

One of the pioneers of that work is Martin Rossman who does what some call hypnosis, although it is actually a light altered state of consciousness – a higher state of consciousness. Other excellent books in this field are "Staying Well with Guided Imagery" by Belleruth Naparstek, and "Healing with Form, Energy and Light," by Tenzin Wangyal Rinpoche, a Tibetan Buddhist.

I've worked with many indigos who were ashamed of their gifts and just wanted to be normal. They try to suppress their energy and capacity. They can easily become depressed or act out as a result. I highly recommend that you practice using the information in this section to help you heal your shame and your child's.

Since we all carry some degree of shame, I'll give you an exercise now to help you heal some of the shame you carry. You can then use it with your children. In my experience, the most effective energy to burn away shame is the use of a violet flame. This visualization is too powerful to heal most issues, so I recommend that you don't use it indiscriminately. However, it's very effective to resolve shame and other major difficulties. Remember, it's not important to actually see the visualization. What's important is your intention and focus.

Exercise:

Let's focus on shame that we all carry from our childhood, whether we're aware of it or not. The more precisely you focus on a specific age and source the better.

Now, focus on your childhood between the ages of ten and fifteen. Think of a shaming interaction that you experienced as a result of your body's development. Now, think of the following questions. Did anyone comment on the following?

- Your budding breasts or bit of fuzz on your chin, and did you feel shamed by that?

- Kids commenting on your "tits" or "boobs." Do you still refer to your breasts by those derogatory terms?

- That you were uncoordinated as a result of growing very quickly?

- Did your mother or father tell you to dress modestly, in a way that felt shaming?

- *Being too smart or knowing too much? Or not being smart enough?*

- *For being too cool or not cool enough?*

- *For having your own opinion? Or for standing up for yourself?*

- *Were you put down for being a "nerd," a "geek," a "dweeb," a "Paki," a "frog," or any other demeaning name-calling based on your looks, interests, religion, or nationality?*

When you're ready, close your eyes. Imagine light coming in from above through the top of your head, your crown chakra. Imagine it as a violet flame. Remember, you don't need to actually see it or feel it.

Imagine the violet flame entering and burning away the shame around your body.

Think of shame as binding your body, making you smaller – and you're burning away those limitations. It's right next to your body, in the first layer of your energy field, the etheric layer of your aura, about two inches (five centimeters) thick.

Burn away the shame that's in your mind as well as around your body. If you have difficulty with your body image – if you're concerned that you're too fat or too thin or too tall or too short, or whatever it is that dissatisfies you about your body, let the violet flame burn away the shame around those aspects.

Burn away the negative energy of the people who shamed you. Shame is an emotion as well as a thought, and it is primarily a dense energy. There are three levels of shame to burn away – the shame around your body, the shame in your third chakra in the area of your solar plexus, and the shame at the mental level – beliefs like "I'm good for nothing."

If someone told us these things repeatedly, or we've repeated these negative messages to ourselves frequently, they become thought forms. These energetic disturbances remain in the third layer of our aura, two feet above our heads. Transform those with violet light as well.

Now check to see how you feel. Check your three vehicles – how are you emotionally, mentally, and physically? How does your energy feel?

Most people say they feel lighter when I use this and other types of healing energy with them. Feeling lighter is one of the essential goals of my work with energy.

These methods don't work with everyone, however. Try it for yourself. Be aware of what you experience. Don't put yourself down if you don't feel any different. That would just be adding more shame to the "collection."

Interestingly, some people are closed to their own experience and don't feel that they're being healed. This doesn't mean that the healing hasn't happened. I can feel the negative energy coming out of them when they do the healing work with me. Others simply prevent themselves from being healed because they believe, unconsciously, that they don't deserve it.

If you don't feel anything, practice becoming more sensitive to your energy and inner experience. Some suggestions to experiment with include the following: focus on your breathing for a few minutes, simply noticing an awareness of the breath going in and out of your body. Also, rub your hands together for a few seconds, then move them slightly apart and feel the magnetic pull of energy between them.

Healing shame and transforming the negative energy that they carry from others are two areas that most people haven't healed, no matter how many books they've read, or how many workshops or healing sessions they've attended.

Shame is a core issue and an approach to healing that I must teach to most of my clients and workshop participants, no matter how many helpers they've seen. That probably applies to you, too. If this exercise worked for you, I encourage you to keep doing it. Each time you do it, focus on another aspect of your life, a different age, another aspect of body dissatisfaction, or any other situation of having been shamed in your life. Remember that shame also comes through our DNA from our ancestors as well as from our past lives.

After you feel some level of confidence and satisfaction with this exercise, I recommend you teach it to your indigo child or youth. The same applies to the other exercises in this book.

Are you one of the people reading through this section who didn't bother trying the exercise? If this is what you did, ask yourself why. What stopped you? What thoughts or feelings did you notice? For some it's pride: *"There's nothing wrong with me, nothing to heal."* For others it's fear: *"What if something shows up I don't like? It'll make me feel bad."* Others simply feel unworthy and repeatedly sabotage themselves.

If you were trying to help your child or one of your friends, you'd probably show them kindness and compassion. I suggest you show the same kindness and compassion to yourself and give yourself the opportunity to resolve shame issues by trying the exercise, even if only for five or ten minutes. After that, you'll be a in a better position to help your child to heal, and you'll have had direct experience on how to do it.

If the methods discussed here don't seem to work for you, I recommend you use methods that have worked for you in the past, and try the other exercises offered in this book. Not every method works for everybody. But be aware that you may have some defenses or feelings that you don't deserve to grow that block you. I will discuss later how we block our own growth. If you have major blocks to growing, whether they're conscious or not, you may need to work with a helper who is experienced in energy psychology or energy psychotherapy.

As an example, I worked with an indigo young woman who had been out in the world selling her photography, and had been very successful. She then returned to live with her family for a year. Her family continued to shame her as they had done when she was child. They told her that she shouldn't rely on her photography to make a living. This shaming and doubt eroded her confidence. I used the healing methods I discussed above with her to help resolve the negativity. She then felt much better and was able to get on with her life successfully again.

Chapter 8
Guilt

It's interesting that some indigos are not affected by guilt in a major way, whereas others are terribly guilt-ridden. On the other hand, a large portion of sensitive souls other than indigos are greatly impacted by guilt.

People "make us feel guilty" for having made a mistake, or at least for having done something wrong in their eyes. The reality, of course, is that we already carry the guilt inside us, and they trigger and amplify it.

Guilt is also self-imposed, as when we judge ourselves for having made a mistake or done something we feel is wrong in relation to another person. Guilt relates to the mind and heart. We *think we hurt someone and this gives us pain in our heart.* It's also a relationship issue, as you'll see with the next story.

The mother of Samuel, a four-year-old indigo, tells him, "Samuel, you make me feel really bad when you say you hate me." With that statement, she makes him responsible for how she feels. The result is that Samuel may spend the rest of his life feeling responsible for other people's emotions, and that his feelings make them feel bad. He learns that it's best to suppress his feelings. However, being a strong-minded indigo, he may become angrier and more rebellious than would a normal child.

One of the differences between guilt and shame is that, with the latter, you often can do nothing to change the difficulty – such as being from the "wrong race," having an overly large nose, or being labeled as bad in your core.

You can do something about guilt though, by talking about it with the other person or through other means. Just as with shame, anger, and fear, guilt is used for social control. People throw these emotions at us partly to control us. Some groups, such as Jewish people and Catholics, specialize in guilt as a form of control by the parents and the church and synagogue. Some Jewish mothers are famous for giving messages to their child like this: _"You don't appreciate your poor mother when I put all this energy into cooking for you,"_ or, _"You only ate two full plates of this meal."_ The same applies to some Ukrainian babas. The grandma says, _"What's the matter, you don't love me enough to eat more of what I made for you?"_ The bottom line is that some cultures specialize in using some emotions more than others – in this case, guilt.

I grew up as a French Canadian Catholic, and was told that I had original sin and needed to be saved by a priest, who was the intermediary for Christ. I was told that I was powerless to do anything to resolve the situation myself.

This was very disempowering and shaming for me, and I spent much of my life feeling guilty, powerless, ashamed, and inadequate, as many Catholics do. The result of these damaging messages by my church was that I left the Catholic faith as a teen, although its negative imprints remained in me to be healed later.

Healing these cultural issues is very important. For example, many traditional First Nations groups did not believe in controlling or punishing a child. What they did instead was to use shame and guilt in the form of ridicule. They would laugh at the child for acting inappropriately. Many First Nations parents still do this, although this parenting approach no longer works. The parents then lose control of their child. As a result, many aboriginal youth become lost souls. As I mentioned earlier, only 31% of aboriginal youth in my city completed high school until recently. Many of them live lives of hopelessness and turn to alcohol and drugs.

All of us need to review the parenting practices that we learned as children to ensure that they aren't damaging for our children.

It's very common for people, particularly sensitive souls, to internalize the guilt. When something goes wrong, those of us who've been given shame and guilt as children are likely to treat ourselves and others in the same way throughout our adult life.

One of the best ways to resolve guilt comes from the twelve-step program of Alcoholics Anonymous. It and other related programs use life review and forgiveness as major aspects to growth, along with asking for help from our higher power. Those are very useful steps to help resolve guilt and shame, and have helped to heal tens of thousands from addictions and other major difficulties. However, the program is designed in a way that keeps people labeled as alcoholics for the rest of their lives. This is meant to be a way of keeping them away from the addictive substance. Although it helps people stay clean and sober, the label is shaming and keeps them in box, always at the risk of relapse.

Exercise:

This exercise is from ancient Hawaii and it's wonderful for resolving guilt. It's called Ho'oponopono. There are four lines with which you address the Creator regarding suffering that you or your relatives or your ancestors have caused, as well as suffering that you see around you. The lines are as follows:

I'm really sorry.

Please forgive me.

I love you (unconditionally).

Thank you (for the forgiveness).

Simply repeat these four statements a number of times. You can use them for a specific issue or repeat them in general.

As an example, I sometimes use my prayer beads, 108 beads, to say this prayer – one per bead. For more information on this technique, refer to "Zero Limits" by Joe Vitale and Ihaleakala Hew Len.

Chapter 9
Self-Hatred and Hatred of Life

Self-hatred is a difficulty experienced by many indigos that I've worked with. However, in my experience, hatred of life is a more common concern among indigos than is self-hatred. These are crucial issues, not only for indigos, but for other sensitive souls as well.

Self-hatred is closely related to shame, but is not the same thing. At the extreme, self-hatred and hatred of life can lead to suicide. When less extreme, they often lead to withdrawal, apathy, self-sabotage, or not bothering to put any effort into the work being done.

Parents, teachers, and professional helpers involved with indigos who express self-hatred and hatred of life sometimes take it personally or feel the troubled indigo just doesn't care. It's more painful when indigos very strongly express this hatred of life directly toward their parents. "I hate you!" coming from our child is very painful to hear.

Loved ones and other helpers may react to the indigo's expression of these feelings by judging or disconnecting from the troubled indigo. This reinforces the indigo's feelings that *"I'm a failure," "life sucks,"* or *"there's no point in trying."*

Over the course of my own healing and in work with many clients over time, I've identified a number of reasons for self-hatred and hatred of life. For example, self-hatred can come from having been victimized. When we're vulnerable, it's easy to take on the labels that abusers give us, but we also take on their negative energy. For example, if someone called us a "loser" when we were young, we can internalize that belief and call ourselves a loser all our lives. However, we also carry the negative energy that accompanied the message in our energy field, three feet (one meter) around us. Also, the other person's attacks can result in holes in our aura, which make us more vulnerable to other attacks in the future.

To resolve self-hatred or hatred of life, the causes of these feelings and perceptions need to be identified and dealt with directly. To harangue people who are caught up in this negativity only makes things worse because they don't know how to resolve it, and they may not even be aware that they carry this negativity. Instead, the difficulties must be healed directly, rather than through denial or blame. The problem is that many parents and other adults are often unable to relate to these deep feelings of negativity carried by indigos and other sensitive people.

As a first step to increasing your understanding and empathy towards your troubled indigo, recognize the various reasons for self-hatred and hatred of life. The following is a summary of reasons for self-hatred. I'll discuss each one of them in the following chapters.

I recommend you engage in the exercises yourself first. Allow yourself to experience the exercise even if the reason seems to have little or no relevance for you. Just experiencing the exercise will give you the capacity to be a stronger support for your troubled indigo. You may also end up feeling better yourself after doing the exercise as a result of transforming negativity that you weren't aware you were carrying.

Reasons for Self-Hatred and Hatred of Life

1. Stinkin' thinkin' – negative self-talk such as, *"I hate myself"*;

2. Loss and depression;

3. Feeling abandoned or unwanted;

4. Feeling judged and harassed by others;

5. Feeling burdened or depleted as a result of negativity from the world;

6. Carrying other people's negative energy – which, as we saw earlier, refers to others' suffering entering into our energy field, just as cigarette smoke does;

7. Death energy – carrying the energy of a person who passed over, part of us dies with them. This also

refers to energy from our coming close to dying as a result of illness when we were younger;

8. Negative effects of medication;

9. Illness and chronic pain;

10. Patterns from previous generations – this refers to attitudes and energy that we pick up from our parents and ancestors, and which affect our DNA – historical trauma;

11. Negative thought forms, which refers to either someone being angry toward us or having another negative emotion or judgment toward us; is like a dark cloud over our heads. This energy is about two feet over our head, in the mental layer of the aura;

12. Curses, which refers to a ritualized curse, like voodoo;

13. Entities, which refers to "ghosts" or other negative energy from the dark side of the universe;

14. Past life issues; and

15. Victimization.

Let's discuss some of these issues now.

1. Stinkin' Thinkin'

This term comes from the field of substance abuse. It refers to our negative self-talk, such as, "I hate this job." This reason for experiencing hatred of life is one which the field of psychology has been working with since its inception and for which useful methods have been developed that help to resolve the issue. Approaches from cognitive behavior therapy are quite helpful for this, although other approaches, such as the ones in this book, are much quicker and deeper. A book from that field which is quite helpful is "Feeling Good" by David Burns. Another excellent author in this field is Albert Ellis.

If you have any amount of "stinkin' thinkin'," I recommend you try the following exercise drawn from cognitive therapy. Cognitive therapy has been well-researched in terms of its effectiveness in helping with depression. It deals with the negative thoughts but not the negative energy. This is why it takes so long to make progress with this method and why many people who try it don't improve.

Exercise:

Take a sheet of paper and divide it in half. On the left side, write one of your negative thoughts. For example, "I'm really stupid." On the right side, list opposing facts to that belief. For example, "I never failed a grade." If the negative feeling is still there, write it down again, and then write another accurate, opposing statement on the right side. Keep going until you feel better. Once the negative statement feels resolved, list another negative one and repeat the process. See the example on the following page.

Stinkin' thinkin' negative belief	Opposing positive fact
I'm really stupid	Actually, I never failed a grade
I'm really stupid	I'm good at my job
I'm really stupid	I love my abilities to do math and to remember names.
I'm ugly	I have attractive eyes
I'm ugly	People often tell me I have a great smile

Keep writing these down until there are no negative statements left in you. I recommend you do this exercise a number of times. The following times you do it, you're likely to have fewer and fewer negatives. Putting your attention on the positive aspects of yourself changes your self-perception. It's a wonderful, simple way to counteract low self-esteem and self-hatred, although using only this exercise is likely to be insufficient.

This method is somewhat similar to making use of affirmations. When using affirmations, you keep repeating a statement such as "I love myself," and hope that the affirmation will eventually sink in. This may work if you don't have serious difficulties. In my personal experience, doing an affirmation like that when I was younger only made me feel worse because I carried too much self-hatred. My self-hatred stemmed in part from the belief that I was a burden, that I shouldn't have been born. The affirmation I later gave myself that was helpful was: "I love you the way you are, you're okay the way you *are*." This was indirect enough to bypass my negative perceptions and feelings toward myself.

Another method that's been used extensively to help resolve negative self-esteem is client-centered therapy by Carl Rogers, a method that's regularly taught in counseling programs. As discussed earlier, it focuses on giving non-possessive warmth and non-judgment to clients. It's important for you to use these on yourself and your indigo child.

Some interesting research regarding this issue was done by Don Andrews, one of my university professors. He did the research with a group of lay counselors who used this method with a group of delinquents. The research included using a group of students trained in counseling methods as helpers. One group of counselors used the supportive Rogerian method with a selected group of delinquents, including being non-judgmental. Another group of counselors told the delinquents they worked with that, although they valued their clients, they disapproved of their behavior. The result showed that those who disapproved of the misbehavior were more helpful to the delinquents. On the other hand, gentle helpers who were non-judgmental of the delinquents were influenced more than their clients. These counselors ended up developing negative attitudes that were similar to those of the delinquents. On the other hand, the delinquents felt better about themselves, but did not change their behaviors whatsoever. This shows that it's important for us to love our indigos unconditionally, but that it's important to state clearly that we don't approve of certain of their behaviors.

I've found that using energy psychotherapy and healing visualizations is much more effective in helping to resolve self-hatred than either cognitive therapy, client-centered therapy, or other Western methods. Energy psychology and healing visualizations are very effective as long as they're focused precisely on the causes of the self-hatred. It's quite useless to try to resolve self-hatred by transforming shame if the cause of "stuckness" is actually something else, such as carrying curses or our parents' negative energy. You can increase your assessment skills and your ability to heal yourself and others if you learn either to use a pendulum or applied kinesiology, otherwise known as muscle testing.

Exercise:

Write down your three favorite ways of putting yourself down. Then with each one, do the butterfly hug as I explained on page 135, four times each.

Tap the index finger and thumb together on one hand three to five times, and then the other hand. Alternate back and forth between your hands while you do the exercise.

Then say: "Even though I _____, I deeply and completely accept myself (and God loves me unconditionally)."

Evaluate and do the exercise again, if necessary. With negative statements that you use frequently, you may need to break the negative belief down into smaller pieces. For example, "I hate myself whenever I make a mistake."

2. Unresolved Grief

Unresolved grief can take many forms. A child who is grieving may withdraw, become clingy, or regress to an earlier age – such as wetting the bed after not having done so for a few years.

We can be challenged with difficulties at any of the emotional phases of the grieving process, which includes the following emotions:

- Denial;

- Bargaining;

- Anger;

- Depression; and

- Acceptance.

We go up and down this range of emotions as we do our grieving. They don't get resolved in a smooth sequence. We can suffer from unresolved grief regarding a variety of issues, such as the loss of a family member or a friend who moved away, loss of a job, loss of a home due to financial difficulties, loss of status at work, and so on.

Unresolved grief is an affair of the heart. Some people stay stuck in one of these emotions for years or decades. The central goal here is for us and our child to go through the unhealed emotions and heal them. Many children resolve their pain and trauma through play, such as playing with dolls, painting, etc. You can help them do that, and talk it through with them. To do this, you could choose to go on the internet and learn methods of play therapy to use with your child.

To do this, one of the options for you or for an indigo who is ten or older is to write a letter to the person or object you're grieving. You will not want to mail it if you're venting negative emotions such as anger and blame. Tell the person what you miss about them and what you valued, as well as what you resented about them.

If the person has died, it's very useful to visit the cemetery and have a talk with the dearly departed there. Tell them what's still in your heart. Let it pour out. Imagine that the person who died is in a higher, wiser place and gives you forgiveness and compassion, and asks for your forgiveness.

The same applies with different forms of loss. Along with the examples mentioned above, this could include loss of a child through an abortion or miscarriage, loss of an arm from an accident, or loss of a large sum of money or other financial assets. For a child, it can relate to such issues as failing a grade, not being accepted in a hockey team, a friend moving away, or losing a pet.

Our unresolved emotions block the free flow of our energy. We need to do our grieving before we can move on to other things. You might need to forgive yourself or ask God to forgive you if you feel you did something wrong to cause the loss.

Many old souls and indigos I've worked with have needed to forgive God for previous losses in this and other lifetimes, although they're usually not aware of their anger toward God. There's often also a parallel feeling of being unworthy of God that we need to work through.

Unresolved loss through separation or divorce can be more complicated. Here, there are negative emotions between the spouses. This complicates the relationship between the adults, as well as between each parent and the child, resulting in the child being caught in the middle. If you'd like more information about the various aspects of family breakdown, you may wish to visit my website that focuses on this issue. It provides free chapters from my book, "Out of Bed & Into the Fire: Damage Control During Relationship Breakdown." My website on this topic is at www.intothefire.ca.

Story:

When my mother died when I was 22, I felt as though I had killed her, although I fully realized at the conscious level that this was nonsense. I had bicycled across much of Canada while she was ill with leukemia. I then chose to live in solitude for six months on a spiritual retreat. She died while I was living in solitude. I discovered later that she had been waiting to see me before she died. I experienced a great deal of self-hatred because I hadn't gone home to be with her before she died. I tried many different methods to heal this. The only thing that helped somewhat was to visit her gravesite and talk to her, although this took several visits over a number of years. It also helped to ask God's forgiveness for my having been so insensitive to her needs and for believing that I had killed her.

If energy psychotherapy had existed when my mother died in 1972, I would have done the butterfly hug, described earlier. I could have said, among other things, "Even though I torture myself by believing that my mother's death was my fault, I deeply and completely accept myself and God loves me unconditionally."

As another example, I could have done a healing visualization, imagining my mother coming to me and telling me that I was not responsible for her death. It would have helped to imagine her giving me a hug as well.

As you can see, and as you may know from your own personal experience, our unconscious beliefs can make life hell for us. Our beliefs, conscious or not, have the ability to sabotage our lives, even to the point of making us physically ill. Taking a drug to avoid the bad feelings only dulls the feelings and prevents us from healing what really ails us. The unconscious patterns still continue to damage our lives.

Chapter 10
Loss and Depression

There are a variety of theories about depression. Drug companies and physicians see it as a metabolic/hormonal phenomenon that requires medication. Cognitive therapists see it as the result of negative thinking. Marriage therapists see it as being the result of relationship difficulties. In fact, depression often stems from a combination of these, and therefore may require a number of different solutions to resolve it. However, as I discussed earlier, medication is not necessary in most cases in my experience because the brain chemicals become rebalanced when we resolve our underlying issues.

Please be aware that depression is more difficult to treat than many other types of difficulties and has a lower success rate, when using traditional Western forms of psychotherapy. As you'll remember from our earlier discussion, the success rate for psychotherapy and counseling is, on average, 68%

to 72%. This varies a great deal depending on the issue being worked with, the client, the helper, the context, and so on.

Gerrig and Zimbardo provided a meta-analysis of the research on psychotherapy with depression in 2008, in which they summarized the results of all well-done research on the treatment of depression over the years.

In this meta-analysis, it was found that for people who take a placebo, 30% improve. A placebo is a sugar pill taken by the patient without their being informed that it's not medication. About 36% improve through psychodynamic psychotherapy. These are derivatives of Freud's methods for attaining insight into personal difficulties. About 52% of patients who take medication improve. Many people who take medication end up with side effects, whether they improve or not. Fifty percent improve with the help of cognitive therapy. Finally, about 52% improve with the use of interpersonal therapy – couple and family therapy.

The most difficult type of depression has been found to be endogenous depression, which refers to long-term depression beginning in childhood. During the years that I worked as a traditional therapist, I was not able to be helpful with most clients who suffered from this type of depression. This is typical for the field of psychology and psychotherapy.

In my practice using holistic healing techniques, I'm now able to help resolve many of the cases of long-term depression within a few sessions, although it takes quite a few sessions for more complex cases, such as people who've experienced extensive abuse or neglect.

If we think of the negativity as stuck or blocked energy, then we can simply resolve it by transforming the sludge. However, we have to identify what that unresolved energy is. Based on my experience over the years, I've come to see depression as often being anger that we've suppressed. Rather than expressing anger outwardly, we attack ourselves with negative judgment. This often occurs to people who want to be very nice. Some of them often feel victimized, feeling attacked or badly treated by others rather than standing up for their rights and concerns. The result is that they also suppress righteous indignation, which is also a part of anger, but is very healthy. The result of suppressing all this is that they give up their personal power in the process.

Exercise:

If you feel even mild depression on occasion, try to get in touch with your underlying anger. You can do this by exploring the variety of emotions that are underlying your self-criticisms. Think of these negative statements as having the benefit of keeping you smaller so that you will keep the peace in the world. Don't knock yourself down for having them.

Whether you're depressed right now or at any other time, I recommend you try the following: Imagine violet flame coming in from above through the top of your head and have it go everywhere – your mind, emotions, and body, as well as your aura, three feet (one meter) around you.

Feel the petty side of your depressive energy and anger being cleansed away with the element of water, down through your feet and into the earth. You can choose to imagine a shower washing this away. Make sure you also cleanse your liver, which is on the left side of your ribs, where anger is stored.

Feel the righteous indignation at the base of your spine, at your first chakra. Have that energy go into your legs, and turn that into more power in your legs. And finally, feel this power go up to your heart center. Feel more power in your heart. Keep practicing this. As you do so, you will gradually feel an increase in your own personal power. Our personal power helps us to feel strong inside and to be less vulnerable to every little bit of negativity that comes our way, so that we can accomplish our goals. It will also help us to stand our ground when necessary, not to push others around or get caught up in ongoing conflict.

Multitudes of old souls work at healing themselves and avoid their personal power like the plague, thus guaranteeing that they will make little progress. A combination of being in our heart and in our power is crucial for true personal growth. If you want to know more about being in your power as opposed to using force, you may want to read "Power vs. Force" by David Hawkins. The book of his that I most highly recommend, and one of my very favorite books, is "Transcending the Levels of Consciousness." Although difficult to read because he's quite abstract, this material will be very useful for you and your indigo.

Part of the issue with depression is that it makes us "smaller." The exercise I just gave you is one of the things you can do to help you regain your personal power quickly. Watch for self-sabotage with this – there may be a big part of you that rejects being in your power.

You can also choose to use the butterfly hug, described on page 135. You would say, "Even though my situation with ____ depresses me, I deeply and completely accept myself (and God loves me unconditionally)." Say this four times for each specific issue. For example, you would say it if your child's acting out drags you down, if your work is stressful, if your connection with your friend is currently going poorly, etc.

If your child carries negativity and is unwilling or unable to do it for themselves because of their age, you can do it on their behalf. Say for them: "Even though I ____, I deeply and completely accept myself and God loves me unconditionally." Say it four times, but be as precise as possible about the issue.

With the healing visualization I offered above, the goal is not simply to get rid of negative energy, but to build up new, more powerful energy. It's very easy to cleanse away old negativity once you know how, particularly if you know precisely what needs to be resolved.

You can have some success in transforming anger in general from your energy field, although it's more powerful to focus on specific issues, such as anger toward your mother because she wasn't there for you when you were small.

Some people go through a cycle of depression, venting anger, feeling guilty, suppressing the anger, being depressed again, etc. If this fits for you, you also need to transform the guilt from darkness to light. In any case, resolve the reasons why you don't allow yourself to feel your anger. You don't need to blast people with it – just feel it and transform it. Then you can assert your perceptions to the other person if it feels appropriate to do so, but do so in a respectful manner.

With healing visualizations regarding a very specific issue, you only have to do it once, and then the negativity is gone forever. There may be other layers to transform later, or you may absorb more of the same energy from the people around you, such as from a depressed spouse. In that case, you simply repeat the healing visualization on a regular basis and put up protective energy.

Building up new energy involves giving yourself permission to be more powerful and to take more space in life. It's like going to the gym – you can't expect to build up new muscles by going once. You have to keep at it and build gradually. Your energy field can only take so much new light at a time. Of course, building up personal power will not work at all if you believe, consciously or unconsciously, that power or connection with Spirit is bad.

When people are in a deep depression, they find it hard to get out of bed and be active in day-to-day life. They're often not in a position to do healing visualizations and other methods that require a certain level of energy to engage in the healing technique.

In some cases of deep depression, the person will need a helper to do the healing work for them to begin with. Starting with methods of healing such as Reiki, homeopathy, and massage may be very useful in such cases.

I've done healing work over the phone with clients and that can work very well also. In other cases, medication may be required. However, as discussed earlier, medication has come to be hugely over-prescribed. Many people don't yet realize the benefit of investing in doing their own work or are afraid to face their own issues.

For those of you who've been sexually abused, being grounded in our power and being in our hearts can be very difficult. However, it's crucial to develop these capacities. Be patient and kind to yourself on your healing journey. Give yourself time for repeated practice of the healing visualizations to grow in your capacity to stay grounded, in your power, and be in your heart. Use the exercises that fit best for you and forget about the rest.

Many women try to be too nice, to help and please, and they give their power away in the process. The goal is for them to go more fully into their power while also retaining their niceness, to be used when appropriate – gentle strength. On the other hand, the goal for many men should be to go more fully into their hearts. There are exceptions to this rule of course – for example, some men are very gentle and need to become more fully in their power. From my perspective, the goal for both males and females is to develop a combination of gentle strength. This is one of the aspects of developing God and Goddess energies in us. Doing this relates to the course I teach called "Profound Healing and Ensouling."

Exercise:

Repeat to yourself, out loud or quietly:

*"Gentle strength. Gentle strength.
Gentle strength..."*

In the case of depression based on relationship issues, it's best to heal this by focusing on relationship work. I'll discuss relationship issues briefly in the last section of this book and more thoroughly in a future book.

In the case of indigo children and youth, they can pick up the depression of the people around them. For example, if a mom has post-partum depression, her baby will be directly affected. She may resolve it within a couple of months but the baby will continue to carry the depressive energy. In this case, you clearly cannot talk to the baby to help it resolve the negativity and you don't want to give it anti-depressants.

Exercise:

If your child carries this depressive energy, I recommend that you have the violet flame enter from above and into your heart center, in the center of your chest. Have the light go to your baby and burn away the depressive energy that it carries in its aura – three feet (one meter) all around its body. If you were sad or depressed prior to delivering your baby, I recommend you do the same at the cellular level. Give your child a great deal of touch and nurturance over the next few weeks.

If you have a teenager who's depressed, think through whether they're carrying your depression from the past or anyone else's, or any of the other energies discussed here. Transform your child's energy in the same way. Then nurture your child or youth in a way that's acceptable to them.

Chapter 11
Judgment

In his book "The Four Agreements," Don Miguel Ruiz discusses how from very early childhood, we have all come to feel unworthy and constantly judge ourselves for our negative thoughts and behaviors, resulting in our trying to keep ourselves in line in order to try to be acceptable to the people around us. Phew – hard work!

Being judged by others also puts a huge burden on us. We know from research, for example, that youth who are given a psychiatric label often end up believing that this is who and what they are – such as oppositional defiant disorder, bully, or learning disabled. They then act in such a way as to confirm that label. This applies to the rest of us too.

One of the options to resolving judgment from other people is to reclaim your power from the people who labeled you and diminished and shamed you, whether they intended to do so or not.

Now let's do an exercise to transform some of these negative beliefs that we all carry, whether we're aware that we do so or not.

Exercise:

Imagine a violet flame coming in from above. Imagine the light two feet (two-thirds of a meter) above your head, at the mental layer of your aura. Imagine it burning away the negative thought forms that some of us carry there. Have the light go into your mind and burn away judgment there. Then burn away the shame that's related to these thoughts, by taking the violet flame in the first two inches (five centimeters) next to your body.

We also judge others, just as they judge us. Rarely are any of us in a place of unconditional love for everything and everyone. We can judge ourselves, our loved ones, God, other people, etc. Some of us have only a mild dose of this, whereas others judge themselves and others on a regular basis. Some of you may remember the book in the 1970s that focused on judgment called "I'm OK You're OK" by Thomas Harris, in which he spoke of four types of people, each with their own type of relationship dance. Here they are, beginning with those who have a low degree of judgment:

- I'm ok, you're ok;

- I'm ok, you're not ok;

- I'm not ok, you're ok; and

- I'm not ok, you're not ok.

By shaming, blaming, and judging others, we add to the negativity in the world. It's also emotionally abusive. We do to others what has been done to us. Use the exercise below to remove the patterns of judging others you may hold in your energy field.

Exercise:

We're already enlightened, as various cultures and paths have told us. We just don't realize it. Various traditions tell us that we already have Buddha Nature, Christ consciousness, Krishna consciousness. The main idea here is that we're perfect in our essence. Our inner perfection is simply covered up by obstructions that need to be removed. Think of the Zen Buddhist perspective that all we need to do to be enlightened is to keep clearing away the dust that covers our light.

You can use the following exercise with any type of negativity that you carry. This one is called the Path of Negation.

With the perspective that we're already perfect in mind, try the following: When any type of negative thought, emotion, or sensation comes along, say to yourself – "I'm not this, I'm not that." So for example, as each arises say:

I'm not my fear.

I'm not my distrust.

I'm not my aggression.

I'm not my tiredness.

This method is very useful to help us disconnect from our petty egos, including "stinkin' thinkin'" and other forms of negativity that block our connection with our Source. This method stems from the Path of Negation developed by some advanced souls from Hinduism and Buddhism. For more information on this path, refer to David Godman's "The Teachings of Sri Ramana Maharshi," and Huang Po by John Blofeld in "The Zen Teachings of Huang Po."

Regarding your indigo child, try to remember that you and your child are already perfect in your inner nature, whenever you judge your child or teach your child to judge the world. You won't always catch yourself doing it, but that's okay. Just give it a try and work toward becoming more and more conscious. That's all we can do. Once your child is old enough to understand, let them know that you're aware that it's not appropriate for you to judge them, and also tell them that this is an issue that you're trying to improve.

Let your child know that it's not okay when they judge even though they may have seen you do it a thousand times.

Teach your child how to heal this negativity in themselves with this and other methods. If your child is too small or unwilling, you can do it for them.

Chapter 12
Fear and Anxiety

Interestingly, fear is less common an issue among indigos as it is for other sensitive souls. The reason for this is that they're powerful, which directly results in their being less caught up in fear. However, some indigos do carry a great deal of fear, as discussed below.

Fear

Fear can stem from a number of very specific causes. You may fear something specific such as black cats or failing tests. Another perspective of fear is that, according to "A Course in Miracles," there are only two emotions – love and fear. Based on this perspective, such issues as anger, depression, and shame are all based on fear. As a result, we need to transform not only those emotions but the underlying fear as well. Then, we replace the fear with love.

Fear of dying is the foundation of all fears, although we generally don't think of this fear. Buddhists and Hindus focus extensively on this fear as a way of attaining liberation. From their perspective, life's dramas are all illusion, and you only need to focus on liberation. They've developed a multitude of methods to attain this state over the millennia, too numerous to mention here.

Many of the healing visualizations I use stem from India and Tibet. I've borrowed others from the professional literature on mind/body healing. I've also developed others, mostly through guidance from Spirit. These methods are very powerful and very quick at healing negativity, including fear and anxiety. They make use of our higher self to help us heal.

We have many reasons for fear. For example, we carry negativity from past lives as well as curses, entities, and other negative energies. The exercises below are quite general, although they will be able to assist you to transform most causes of fears. You need to be very specific as to the cause to help you be successful in resolving your fears.

Exercise for fear #1:

Imagine a little cap being put at the top of your head. Now imagine fear being pulled out from throughout your body by the roots. Think of this as assisting to cleanse unresolved past life material that has gone into our body through the crown of our heads from the seat of our souls, six inches (15 centimeters) above our heads.

Exercise for fear #2:

Imagine that you carry a bag of fear at the base of your spine. Have the light go in and wash it down into the earth.

Exercise for fear #3:

Imagine light going into your kidneys, at your back, behind your ribs. Cleanse away fear that is stored in your kidneys.

Exercise for fear #4:

Imagine that the fear stems from your inner child. Put one hand on your heart chakra, at the center of your chest, and your other hand on your belly. Have the light go in from above and into your heart center. Fill it up. Then have the light from your heart center go to your inner child, which is in your belly. You can choose to move your hand to various areas of your belly as you do this. Do this for several minutes.

You can also choose to use the exercise that I mentioned earlier, called the butterfly hug. You'll find it earlier in this section on page 135.

Anxiety

Anxiety is more diffuse than fear – not linked to a specific cause. For example, you may be anxious about everything when you go into crowds or you may wake up anxious.

Anxiety is very common for both indigos and old souls. The reason for this, as mentioned earlier, is that they are highly affected by negativity around them, as well as from their DNA and past lives, whether they realize that or not. This almost certainly results in far more indigos and sensitive souls becoming medicated for anxiety than other people. That's very unfortunate because these issues can be very easily healed when we're able to pinpoint the difficulty and use the right tools.

Since so many people are on medication for anxiety, I'll give you some very specific guidelines to help resolve this issue. However, it's impossible to be all-inclusive because there are so many aspects to these anxiety concerns. Most of these can be resolved very easily if you can identify what they are. This is part of what our courses teach people to do.

In terms of anxiety, I've already discussed secondary and vicarious trauma earlier in this section. These can lead to generalized anxiety. Follow the exercise mentioned in the section on trauma to resolve these.

Exercise for anxiety #1:

Butterfly Hug: *Repeat four times while alternately tapping the index finger and thumb of each hand: "Even though I'm really anxious right now, I deeply and completely accept myself and God loves me unconditionally." Repeat four times. Refer to page 135 of this book for more specific details of this exercise.*

Exercise for anxiety #2:

Healing Visualization: *Imagine light going into the various layers of your aura and transforming the negativity there.*

Exercise for anxiety #3:

Use a violet flame through the crown of your head into your aura to transform the causes of your anxiety.

You may need to be very precise to assess the cause of your anxiety in order to resolve it. You can do this if you learn to assess your energy field with a pendulum or through muscle testing. I teach both in our courses as well as in my sessions with clients, including online. You can probably learn these methods with a healing professional in your area.

It's very important that you learn how to assess these issues if your indigo is very sensitive and easily becomes anxious.

Grounding and protection are very helpful for sensitive souls and some indigos, so they can be less vulnerable to issues that cause fear and anxiety.

Exercise for anxiety #4:

Grounding: *Imagine light transforming obstructions in the first six inches (15 centimeters) below your feet.*

Imagine roots going down into the earth from the base of your spine deep into the earth. Imagine that you become rooted like a big oak tree. This exercise should be done at least once a day, and three times a day for particularly sensitive souls or if you're going through difficult times. The same applies to protection.

Exercise for anxiety #5:

Protection: *There are a variety of forms of protection. Try this one: Imagine a bubble around your body protecting you, three feet (one meter) around from your body. Negative energy cannot enter into you, but your energy can go out. An alternative method is to imagine a layer of rose pink Christ light right next to your body, all around you. This should be two inches (five centimeters) thick.*

Different religions have specific prayers for protection as well. For example, Hindus call on Ganesh, and Catholics have specific prayers for protection.

Chapter 13
Anger

People get angry for a variety of reasons. Some people use anger as a way of controlling other people. They've learned that they can get their way through bullying.

On the other hand, some people who've been victimized distrust people and they take out this negativity on others. Some of the work they need is to heal the victimization.

Others feel anger as a result of being afraid. This is quite common among males who've learned to feel anger and avoid other feelings, including fear. One of the goals for these people is to get in touch with the underlying feelings and heal the related issues. They also need to realize that they might prefer expressing anger because it helps them to feel and be more in control. They need to realize that this is a false sense of security and may actually make things worse. This style of being has been labeled by psychologists as a "Type A" personality. Evidence has shown that Type A's have a higher rate of heart attack than other people. For those of you who are interested in mind-body literature regarding what personality type is likely to result in what type of illness, I recommend "Awakening Intuition" by Mona Lisa Schultz. This is a very useful book. The author has compiled the medical research that explores different illnesses as they correlate with various personality types.

Then there are the Type C personalities, who suppress their anger and become powerless instead. Research has shown that this type is at greater risk of having cancer. A healthier orientation is the Type B personality, who is calmer than Type A and more in their power than Type C.

Another aspect is that anger is a distancer in relationships. What that means is that people are more likely to withdraw from us after we blast them with our anger. The healthier approach is to be in touch with our anger, and after dealing with it internally, speak calmly about our concerns with the other person.

For some people anger is based on righteous indignation or outrage – this is a form of anger that's very common among indigos. They want life to be different and are more likely to express anger directly because they're upset with the way things are. Among other things, some are too aggressive at school and others push their parents or siblings around. They may also be angry at one person and take it out on another.

Indigos will deal more effectively with their righteous indignation if they learn which battles they can fight and which situations to accept. The serenity prayer from

Alcoholics Anonymous mentioned earlier applies very well here:

"God grant me the serenity to accept the things I cannot change, the courage to change the things I can, and the wisdom to know the difference."

Of course, these words will be very difficult for a five- or six-year-old to understand. It's your job as a parent to translate it for your child.

You as a parent or other caring adult can help guide the child toward making the world a better place in an area that the child is concerned about. For example, if a six-year-old child is concerned about pollution, the parent and child can pick up garbage together. If a ten-year-old is concerned about children in Africa, he can save a portion of his allowance or earn money from something like a lemonade stand to give to a cause. Older children can take on bigger responsibilities, such as bringing people with similar concerns together to create an activity, or joining a pre-established group, perhaps with your involvement.

Story:

A ten-year-old, John, carried his father's angry energy. This is an example of anger picked up through secondary trauma. The child learned by age two that he could get his way with his mother if he got angry. His mom had learned to be afraid of anger when she was a child because her mother

> would fly into rages and hit her. John was sent from one professional to another to resolve the issue. There was little success, partly because his mother thought the problem was solely in her child, and looked for help accordingly. She tried child counselors, naturopaths, and school counselors. What actually needed to be resolved was the mother's trauma from her own childhood, in addition to resolving the negativity that John had picked up from his father. If the father had been available at the time of working with the child, it would have been useful to work on resolving his anger as well.

Another reason why people become angry is frustration that their needs aren't being met. For example, a child with learning disabilities will likely become frustrated and angry in class because he doesn't understand. And a boy with a great deal of energy who has to sit at his desk all day can easily become fidgety and angry, and even become labeled as a problem child, although the real problem is with the educational style. This is why far too many boys drop out of high school before graduation. Research also shows that more females go to university now than males do.

If the frustration is with another child at school, your child needs some coaching on how to handle the situation. I suggest you start by helping your child express her negative feelings, and then understand where her schoolmate may be coming from, so that she can hopefully develop compassion for the other child. Then you can bounce ideas around in terms of what might be helpful for your child to do.

As a result of the Dalai Lama's efforts and those of Daniel Goleman, author of "Emotional Intelligence," many programs are being established around the world to teach children compassion and emotional intelligence. I suggest you look into what's being done in your child's school about this. If they don't have a program to help children develop these skills and address such issues as bullying, I recommend you ask that a program be brought in. If they ignore your request, connect with other parents, and ask again as a group. There's power in numbers. It may be most useful to ask at the school board level if your school doesn't respond.

If your child is frustrated and angry regarding math homework, you may want to consider whether they have a learning disability, or if they simply need more time than is allowed in class to deal with their questions about the math assignment. If your child hates a particular school project, perhaps working on it for five or ten minutes at a time and taking breaks could work very well. In other cases, a reward after completing an assignment might be useful.

It's part of a parent's role to ensure that the tasks the child has to deal with are not too difficult and overwhelming, as well as not too simple and boring. If your child is angry with a teacher on a regular basis, it's your job as a parent to find out what's going on and determine with the teacher what steps to take to resolve it.

Fight or flight is another reason for anger. The child fights because he feels threatened. He may have been traumatized before by math difficulties and failed some tests, and would much rather fight with you than risk another failure.

Anger can also arise if the child has felt rejected from age two, when his little sister was born. He still reacts by picking on her and gets angry when mom and dad *"take her side against him."* Children may also react negatively if they're ostracized at school. This could be related to prejudice or a whole host of other reasons. It's essential that you have a positive relationship to be able to talk with your child to find out what his concerns are.

When helping a child or an adult struggling with anger, it's essential to help resolve the cause of the anger rather than simply teaching them to cope with negativity. Too many of us have learned as children to cope with injustice rather than take a stand against it, and indigos are less likely to be tolerant of doing this. On the other hand, many sensitive souls are likely to be too tolerant, as a result of fear of conflict. If you wish for more ideas on dealing with anger in your child, you could explore "Anger and the Indigo Child" by Dianne Lancaster.

If you see only the surface issue, you'll be only dealing with the child's behavior though methods such as behavior management. As I mentioned earlier, the reason why fewer people are seeing traditionally trained therapists, and more people are either taking medication or seeing alternative healers, is that their problems are not being resolved. The bottom line is that you must be very clear about the cause before the deeper issue can be healed.

Chapter 14
Bipolar Disorder

Bipolar disorder is defined by the American Psychiatric Association as behavior that alternates between manic and depressive episodes. The individual has had at least one manic episode and more than one major depressive episode. I will not take the time to discuss this label at length except to ask you, dear reader, whether you had emotional ups and downs when you were a teen. Try to remember whether you experienced puppy love, as it used to be called, periods of depression or low self-esteem, and periods of being highly excitable. If these moods were fairly intense at times, you and many of us could have been labeled as having bipolar disorder and been medicated. This label is certainly valid in some cases. However, it's normal for us to have fairly large mood swings, and especially so for teens experiencing dramatic physical, hormonal, emotional, mental, and relationship changes.

The issue of mood swings applies even more to indigos than to the rest of us. Because they're so sensitive, they feel things more strongly than other people do – for better and for worse. For example, I've worked with indigos who've had major reactions to bullying at school, to parental conflict, power lines, and various other issues. Professionals aren't able to find the cause and so they label the issue as being internal rather than having an external cause.

I've worked with many indigos over time who were very disturbed energetically because they had picked up negative energy from various sources. The child is then labeled as bipolar and this limits how they're perceived by parents, teachers, and others. It also limits the children in what they feel they can do. All of this is very damaging to the child.

On the other hand, I've recently been involved with two clients who have a loved one who is deeply troubled and has been labeled as having bipolar disorder. In one case, the woman is in a relationship with a man who keeps withdrawing from her when he's in the depressive phase. Sometimes she doesn't hear from him for many days.

In the other case, I saw a mother recently whose daughter had been labeled as bipolar. From what the mother told me, her daughter was an advanced indigo with very special gifts. However, she was also reported to have been troubled by bipolar episodes much of her life. The woman's husband was also assessed as having bipolar disorder. The woman, in her words, "lived with intense bipolar and was on 'suicide watch' for over 20 years." Her daughter eventually committed suicide when she was 24.

To use the mother's words, "I have been through every healing modality known to our society, in seeking awareness and healing for my daughter's illness and her father's. Over 25 years of living with bipolar, and every avenue of healing imaginable, intuitive, nutritional, shamanic, Native American, mental health work, psychotherapy, medical, and in the few months preceding my daughter's death, psychiatric." She reported that she found peace when her child was labeled as bipolar because this helped them to understand and come to terms with a very difficult situation. From her perspective, the best website on this topic, which covers all aspects of bipolar and depression, is www.mcmanweb.com.

This was clearly a very difficult and painful situation for all concerned. I did not see the father or the daughter and so was unable to assess whether I could have helped the daughter. However, no helper is able to help everyone who asks for help. Even such luminaries as Jesus, Buddha, and Aristotle had people who turned away from them and even turned against them.

However, I'm not a believer in giving up. Despair is our biggest enemy. I've had excellent success in helping to heal many people who have experienced serious and sometimes dangerous mood swings, through my healing work.

SECTION II:

EXTERNALIZED DIFFICULTIES

Externalized Difficulties

The Diagnostic and Statistic Manual (DSM-IV) developed by the American Psychiatric Association discusses both internalizing and externalizing difficulties. There is also a separate category that includes such issues as eating disorders, schizophrenia, and autism. Internalizing difficulties include such issues as anxiety and depression. As we've seen, these states focus inward, and their symptoms and related difficulties have been discussed in the previous chapters.

Externalizing difficulties are behaviors that have a major impact on others. I'll discuss these now. The following are the main categories here: performance difficulties, including ADD (attention deficit disorder) and ADHD (attention deficit and hyperactivity disorder), oppositional defiant disorder, conduct disorder, and self-harm and suicide. As we discussed earlier, far more males have these difficulties than females, whereas far more females have internalized difficulties.

Chapter 15
Performance Difficulties

Performance Difficulties

In the case of the many indigos who've given up on performing, such as doing homework or getting a job, there are a variety of things that need to be done, depending on the situation. In the case of a youth with learning difficulties and ADHD that I worked with, he received mostly negative feedback and very little positive feedback at school. He then ended up feeling like giving up. It is best for a parent in this type of situation to maintain a focus on keeping their relationship with the child as positive as possible because of all the negative attention he receives at school.

Many indigos see schoolwork as being boring and unworthy of their interest. An option in these cases is to negotiate with the teacher so that the child only has to answer one math question on a particular topic, rather than five, when it's clear that the child knows the work.

Other indigos can't be bothered with menial tasks. It's not worth their time because they want to accomplish the big vision and aren't interested in the small steps. They need to be assisted to see that we can only accomplish great things by taking one small step at a time. To explore options with them is also very important, so they can be very clear on how both the vision and the steps they need to take fit together toward the achievement of their goal.

Others have no purpose in life and become lazy or depressed, or they may be reacting against a parent pushing them to be productive. In other cases, their body could be unbalanced because of their diet or some other difficulty. Do they have energy for other things but avoid responsibility, or is their energy simply very low overall?

You as a parent need to determine as clearly as possible why your child is avoiding responsibility if you're to be successful in helping them. Talk to them about it. They may not even know why they're not behaving responsibly.

In terms of healing, a variety of things may need to be done. One example is to help resolve the negative energy in the child relating to school or perhaps getting a job, to help him build on his strengths rather than focus on his weaknesses, to transform the negative energy from darkness to light from a teacher who labeled him, and so on.

If all else fails, I recommend you take the young person to a healer who understands these types of issues and is able to discern the causes, through intuition or muscle testing/ applied kinesiology, which is an invaluable way to ask the body why your child is in difficulty. You can ask many kinds of questions with this. You may want to check in your area to see where you can learn these skills. If these methods don't work, consider distance healing on the youth if he refuses to see the healer.

On the other hand, they may be uninterested in the menu laid out before them. For example, some indigo youth have no interest in local projects but are very interested in helping out in the Third World. It's useful to remember the words of George Bernard Shaw in this context:

"Reasonable people adapt themselves to the world.
Unreasonable people attempt to adapt the world to themselves.
All progress, therefore, depends on unreasonable people."

Chapter 16
ADD and ADHD

Since the issue of ADD and ADHD all too frequently comes up with indigos, I'll discuss this issue in some detail here.

According to the American Psychiatric Association, at least six of the following symptoms need to be present for six months before a diagnosis of ADD or ADHD can be made.

Inattention:

1. Pays little attention to details and makes careless mistakes;

2. Has difficulty paying attention;

3. Does not listen when spoken to;

4. Fails to follow through or finish tasks;

5. Has difficulty getting organized;

6. Avoids tasks requiring sustained mental effort or concentration;

7. Often loses things needed for school or other daily tasks;

8. Is easily distracted; and/or

9. Is often forgetful in daily activities.

Hyperactivity/Impulsivity:

1. Often fidgets or squirms;

2. Often leaves seat when staying seated is expected;

3. Runs about or climbs on things in inappropriate settings;

4. Has difficulty engaging in quiet play or other activities;

5. Is constantly on the go or appears to be driven by a motor;

6. Talks excessively;

7. Blurts out answers prematurely;

8. Has difficulty waiting turn; and/or

9. Often interrupts or intrudes on others.

There are a variety of issues that can impact indigos and other sensitive souls so that they begin to become hyperactive. I recommend that you check all of the following before putting your indigo or other sensitive child on any medication, because this can have such a damaging effect on them. If your child is already on medication, check the following, and then you may decide whether to stop this treatment for a time while you try these methods. You can choose to leave the child on the medications, but the result of the healing work will be lessened because the child's spirit and mind will not be as clear and receptive as they otherwise would be. Many children and youth who are on medication are taken off them during weekends and summers, so this would be a natural time to assess the situation.

Food

Many children are adversely affected by unhealthy foods such as white sugar, white flour, and red dye. Others have various other food and environmental allergies and may have serious negative reactions to them. I strongly recommend you have your child assessed for things of this nature.

In some cases, the child may receive money from the parent for lunch and will spend it on pop and chips, instead of something nutritious, without the parent realizing it.

Family Dynamics

A child can be negatively affected and hyperactive if there's conflict between his parents, or if one or both parents are highly stressed. As examples, a child whose parents divorced when she was three years old became depressed because she felt their separation was her fault. Another felt she was unwanted when she was in the mother's womb. In another case, there's a curse against the family that may span over generations. Although everyone is affected, only the indigo, along with other very sensitive souls, are so sensitive as to be profoundly affected by it. Curses will be discussed in Chapter 20. I'll discuss family-related issues in Part 3 of this book.

School and Community

The label of ADD and ADHD most often comes up for indigos in relation to the school system because most teachers want children to sit quietly and behave. This doesn't work well for indigos, and especially boys. Also, regular schooling focuses on teaching the child facts and figures, in a style which is mostly focused on the left brain – on rational, linear thinking. Most indigos are far more right-brained, which is more focused on visual, spatial, spiritual, holistic, and creative thinking. They generally learn best with hands on, which does not fit with most classes in traditional schools. Hence, it's basically built-in that many indigos will fail in the traditional school system because of the style of teaching that's used there. This is becoming a bigger problem because more and more children are becoming indigos.

Although some school systems are experimenting with alternate forms of teaching, not enough is being done and far too many youth are being labeled as the problem. The real problem is actually the school system. The method of teaching in traditional schools generally brings out the worst in many children, and particularly indigos. I know one school trustee who's trying to create change in her city's school board, but the board is desperately holding on to what they believe is "the tried and true" system. The result is that far more children drop out, are kicked out, or fail because the old guard is holding on to power and trying to maintain the old ways of teaching. Although this will certainly change in time, it's damaging to a great many children today.

Of course, politicians are part of the problem because they need to supply enough money to provide what are often seen as frills, which actually ensure that children remain in school and complete their education. Trying to save money by saving on such "frills" results in many children falling by the wayside, and this ends up costing far more to the government and taxpayers in the long run.

Many different factors can affect a child at school. For example, in some cases a youth can fail a grade or become severely disturbed because he's perceived negatively by a teacher.

In other cases, there are negative energies either inside or outside the child. These can include issues at the DNA level from previous generations, curses, entities, as well as negative energy on the land. Read the last few pages of Part 2 to help you determine if these might be factors for you or your child.

Witnessing bullying or being bullied can result in a child developing symptoms that appear to be ADD or ADHD. Attending a school that carries negative energy is also an important factor. This can take a variety of forms. For example, an elementary school in Vernon, BC, Canada used to be a jail and was then converted into an elementary school. Think of how detrimental the energy would be there for sensitive children and school staff.

In another case, the school is on land where there were many deaths among First Nations people when Europeans invaded their land. In other cases, the energy around the school or the child's home is very negative. These energies all need to be transformed from darkness to light for these very sensitive children to function well.

All of this is not to say that the labels of ADD and ADHD are invalid. I'm simply saying that although the label and medication are appropriate in some cases, in most situations there are factors that are causing the difficulties in the child. It must be determined what is causing the problem, and then resolve it.

Some people recommend that when difficulties arise, the child should be tested by a psychologist. Although there's some validity to this, when my son was tested by a very pleasant and well-meaning psychologist, he was simply labeled and pathologized. Although he was indeed hyperactive in some ways, he was able to focus very well on what interested him and became distracted when something bored him. He also tuned people out when he felt coerced. These issues are very common for many children who are labeled ADD or ADHD, but these issues are also common among indigos.

My recommendation is that you find a psychologist with some degree of spiritual understanding, who knows about indigos, and who is able to take the child's strengths and gifts into consideration when making recommendations. Ask them to give you some examples and a reference or two before you agree to have your child tested by them.

The problem at this point, as research has shown, is that fewer psychologists and other counselors actually believe in God and spirituality than do other people, on average. The majority of helping professionals who do have spiritual beliefs have not integrated this into their practice. Since your indigo is a spiritual being in the physical world, more so than most, these professionals will not be able to help and may make things worse. A helper can only go as far as they've gone themselves.

You as parent need to find someone who has the ability to assess learning disabilities as well as negative energies. Since most helpers are unable to do both, you may need to put on your detective hat and see a variety of professionals to help you determine the cause of your child's or your difficulties.

For more information on ADD and ADHD as it relates to indigos, I recommend you refer to Doreen Virtue's book, "The Care and Feeding of Indigo Children."

I recommend you use the exercises in this book to help resolve the causes of the difficulties.

Chapter 17
Oppositional Defiant Disorder and Conduct Disorder

Oppositional Defiant Disorder

According to the DSM-IV, a person who is labeled as having oppositional defiant disorder must have had the following difficulties for at least for six months, during which at least four of more of the following are present:

1. Often loses temper;

2. Often argues with adults;

3. Often refuses to comply with adults' requests or rules;

4. Often deliberately annoys people;

5. Often blames others for his or her mistakes rather than taking responsibility;

6. Is often easily annoyed by others;

7. Is often angry or resentful; and

8. Is often spiteful or vindictive.

These behaviors must be more intense than the norm, for their age group, to be labeled as ODD. This disturbance has been found to cause clinically significant impairment in academic, social, and occupational functioning.

At least half of the teens I've worked with over the course of my career could have fit these criteria. Is that your experience too? In my view, it's totally inappropriate to label a child as having ODD if they're strong-minded, particularly if they're having a power struggle with adults who are rigid and controlling. The goal in these cases is to help to heal the child's anger and/or resolve the conflict between adult and child. This can be done by working with both people, or by working with the adult only, or the child only. There are many options here. Please don't get caught up in believing that these are hopeless cases. They are only hopeless cases for people who don't know how to handle them and who are not prepared to be open-minded about the child's situation. They mean well, but they have yet to learn some of the skills needed to help your child.

Conduct Disorder

Some people become aggressive toward others or toward property when they're off base. More youth do these things than other people, and a larger proportion of them are male. For example, as research has shown, boys who experience divorce are more likely to become angry and act out their pain, whereas girls will internalize their pain and most likely have relationship difficulties later on. If you wish more information on this, you may refer to my book on family breakdown.

However, the rules have been changing with indigos. With girls and young women being more in their power these days, partly because of women's liberation and partly because of the indigo phenomenon, there has been more destructiveness and aggression from girls and young women in the past 15 years or so. Because they tend to act out their difficulties, many youth with conduct disorders are likely to be indigos. If we treat them as being dysfunctional, they will behave accordingly. As research has shown, people who are given a label, whether depressed, delinquent, or bipolar, are likely to act accordingly to fit the label.

At the beginning of my career, I spent two years working in a group home with troubled youth who had oppositional defiant behavior. We used a model whose central approach was the use of logical consequences, where the punishment fits the crime, so to speak. This worked very well with these young people. We helped them to improve their behavior over a period of two years or more, and they were then sent back home to their families. On returning, because they had changed but the family situations had not, they began acting out again. The parents would then revert back to their old ways of handling them, and an escalating vicious cycle would develop. This is why I returned to school to receive training as a family therapist. After doing family therapy for a number of years in a child protection context in which there was a great deal of parent/child conflict and so-called oppositional defiant disorder, our research found that family therapy was very effective in assisting to resolve those difficulties. I'll say more about this in a future book on indigos and their families.

A wiser and more effective path than labeling indigos and trying to control them is to help them get in touch with their wisdom and spirit and heal from there, and for the parents to learn to handle the situation more effectively. The parents may also need to heal some of their issues for the family to work better. In my experience, this works very well with most of these young people.

However, in some cases, they choose not to be healed. The following is an extreme example of an indigo being very clear about what he wanted and completely ignoring the alternatives, to his detriment.

Story:

A 17-year-old came into my office with his parents. He was referred to me because he had been in detention for having transported illicit drugs for a criminal gang. The interesting phenomenon about this youth was that he'd been bullied in earlier grades. He was traumatized but refused to work at healing this, because it was too scary and painful for him. His solution was to hang out with a very tough gang to help him feel safe. The problem with that was that the gang members were quickly dying off due to warfare between rival gangs – not the wisest place to go for safety.

Following is the list of symptoms for conduct disorder from the DSM-IV.

Aggression towards people and animals:

- Bullies, threatens, or intimidates others;

- Initiates physical fights;

- Uses a weapon that can cause serious physical harm to others (e.g., bat, brick, broken bottle, knife, gun);

- Physically cruel to people;

- Physically cruel to animals;

- Attacks and robs others (e.g., mugging, purse snatching, extortion, armed robbery); and/or

- Rapes - forces into sexual activity.

Destruction of property:

- Commits acts of arson, with the intention of causing serious damage; and/or

- Deliberately destroys property (other than through arson).

Deceitfulness or theft:

- Breaks into houses, buildings or cars;

- Lies to obtain goods or favors or to avoid obligations (i.e., "cons" others); and/or

- Steals items of nontrivial value without confronting a victim (e.g., shoplifting, breaking and entering – without a weapon; forgery).

Serious violations of rules:

- Stays out at night despite parental prohibitions, beginning before age 13;

- Runs away from home overnight at least twice while living in parental or parental surrogate home (or once without returning for a lengthy period); and/or

- Truant from school, beginning before the age of 13.

With these types of difficulties, it's important for the parents to work as a team with each other and with the professionals involved. I recommend that the parents work as a team even if they're separated. However, as research has shown, 25% of divorced spouses are what are termed "fiery foes," who keep fighting for years with the children caught in the middle. For more information on this topic, refer to "The Good Divorce" by Constance Ahrons or to my book on family breakdown.

In those and other situations, many parents are too preoccupied with their own difficulties to help their children get back on track. Some are alcoholics, workaholics, traumatized parents, or people who work two jobs to make ends meet.

In those cases, it's often very important for other involved adults to take some steps to help out, such as:

- Encouraging the parents to develop healthier and more balanced lives, allowing for more time and energy for their child;

- Helping them to vent and to focus differently on their child;

- Providing parents with a break if they're overwhelmed with too many obligations;

- Connecting with the youth directly in a positive manner; and/or

- Providing money for counseling with someone who's likely to be helpful. It should take no more than three sessions to know if a particular helper will be appropriate.

Those trying to help these youth should realize that the youth are feeling unimportant, whether rightly or wrongly, and are acting out their hurt and anger. Others carry negative energies and act them out in the world. Our focus needs to be on gently supporting and containing them, as well as helping them to heal, not on judging them. If counseling is needed and the family is unable to pay and you can't afford to pay for a helper yourself, try raising funds among family members, or seek the help from a professional healer who understand indigos. In some cases, the fee could be covered by a third party, such as an Employee Assistance Program.

Chapter 18
Self-Harm and Suicide

Most people give a warning before they attempt suicide. Males are more likely to complete the suicide attempt successfully. Females tend to make many attempts before finally committing suicide. All warnings should be taken very seriously. Risk is increased if a person is contemplating suicide and also takes alcohol or drugs. Research shows that suicide is the third largest cause of death of American youth aged 15 to 24 (Springen, 2009).

Part of the tragedy is that a person committing suicide has a very negative impact on many people. When a high school student commits suicide, others are more likely to follow suit. It can also be infectious within families. For example, I worked with a family in which a young man killed himself. His brother then made a suicide attempt, although he did not complete it. In another instance, a young woman attempted suicide and then her mother considered suicide as well. In yet another case, two brothers from the same family committed suicide.

It's important for us to think of all thoughts of dying and suicide as being impacted by negative energies that must be transformed, together with feelings of despair and hatred of life. Helping the suicidal person to find purpose is also crucial. In some cases involving youth, they attempt suicide as a form of revenge. This also must be discussed and resolved.

Another useful perspective is that the suicidal person may feel unwanted by people around them, regardless of whether this perception is warranted. This must also be healed. It's important for the suicidal person to become connected with others in a positive way. The family is particularly crucial in this.

In my experience working with people who are suicidal, the vast majority can be assisted to resolve their issues and go on to live happy and productive lives. It's also important to know that in most cases suicidal feelings usually only last a short time. The crucial issue is to help them get over the hump as quickly as possible.

In some cases, they don't want the help. However, we can still send them distance healing, which may help to resolve the issue sufficiently to prevent the suicide.

In the field of family therapy, a suicide watch in which the highly suicidal person is observed 24 hours a day is a method that has been used successfully. This in part shows the suicidal person that they're deeply cared for.

Another option is to ask high beings such as archangels for help. If that appeals to you, check out Doreen Virtue's book on the "Proper Caring and Feeding of Indigos."

I believe that indigos are more likely to consider suicide than other people because they're so sensitive and so easily affected by negativity. They're also more likely to take decisive action on it because they have so much personal power.

If your child or youth or other loved one is talking about suicide, always take it seriously. Seek help from people who know how to handle it. Your child's refusing to see a psychologist or other helper is not acceptable. I believe that we must lose our right to choose whether to see a professional helper when there's either moderate or high risk of suicide. In some cases, they may need to be taken to a hospital to prevent the suicide.

If you want to learn more about this issue, I suggest you read an article called "Daring to Die" by Karen Springen.

You can determine if there is risk of suicide by asking the person the following questions:

- Do they have thoughts of suicide?

- How long have they been thinking about it and why?

- Are they seriously considering doing it?

- Do they have a plan?

- Do they have the means to do it?

- Do they have reasons that would prevent them from carrying it out?

If the risk is moderate or higher, you can try to set a contract with them to not take any suicidal action for a limited period of time. If the risk is very high, it may be best not to leave them alone at all and perhaps take them immediately to a hospital. However, it is not appropriate to be pushy about it.

In addition, behaviors that suggest there's a possibility of suicide can include:

- Putting their affairs in order;

- Taking very high risks, and not caring about the results;

- Discussing suicide or expressing the thought that they don't care about living; and/or

- Losing interest in life or talking about feeling worthless and that life is pointless.

However, feeling worthless or losing interest in life and talking about wanting to die can simply mean that they feel very badly, although they are not planning on killing themselves at all. It's very appropriate to ask if they're suicidal. You do not need to worry that you might put the idea into their head.

If you're concerned about these issues, there are suicide prevention telephone lines and other services in most cities in North America.

I recommend you try to help the suicidal person to work through the exercises in this book in the section on self-hatred and hatred of life, among others. The causes vary from one individual to another and should not all be treated the same. For example, some people want to die because they have too much physical pain, or trauma, or have a mental illness that brings them more pain than they feel they can endure. Others just want to go back to Spirit – *"Why should I have to be here?"*

Self-harm is less final than suicide but is along the same continuum. It also relates to hatred of oneself and of life, as well as disconnection from Spirit, and should be healed accordingly. These issues, along with all the others discussed in this book, should always be looked at as a spiritual difficulty, and possibly also related to mental, emotional, physical, and relationship difficulties.

The Royal College of Psychiatrists has a useful website on self-harm at http://www.rcpsych.ac.uk/ mentalhealthinformation/mentalhealthproblems/depression/ self-harm.aspx. They note that one out of ten young people will self-harm at some point. Women, gays and lesbians, and some sub-cultures, such as "Goths" are more likely to self-harm according to the research they mention.

One person I worked with cut herself or took many pills and needed to be taken to the hospital whenever she became close to a partner. She had a personality disorder that made it too painful for her to have a loving relationship.

Another client I worked with cut herself regularly because she was very numb from having been sexually abused as a child. It was her way of getting in touch with feelings.

Another client cut herself because she had a great deal of emotional pain. It was her way of releasing pain. She had been doing it for years and her family was not aware of it at all, even though she had many scars on her arms. The parents were oblivious to her suffering because they were so caught up in their own.

Many years ago, I wrote a summary of the literature on relationships in families in which there is sexual abuse. One of the aspects was that there's a higher rate of children being sexually abused if the mother has also been sexually abused. These children then hate themselves and hate life, and may act out against themselves.

Some groups have a much higher rate of self-harm than others. For example, aboriginal people in North America and around the world have a much higher rate of suicide, substance abuse, sexual abuse, violence, violent deaths, and other difficulties than the rest of the population. The bottom line for them is that they've been disenfranchised from their connection with the earth and with their spirit. They've also been treated with prejudice. If you're a First Nations individual and this issue resonates with you, feel free to contact me and I will send you a free article and a questionnaire that I've written on aboriginal youth, families, and communities.

As a final word, anorexia and bulimia can also be very life-threatening. One of the aspects of these difficulties is

self-hatred and hatred of life. These issues are discussed
elsewhere in this book.

Chapter 19
Alcohol and Drugs - Legal and Illegal

It's important for you to have some understanding of alcohol and drugs, whether legal or illegal, because so many youth and other sensitive souls get involved with them. However, I'm providing you with only a brief thumbnail sketch of some of the highlights, so please explore other sources regarding this issue. The information provided here and a website I recommend is www.not4me.org, an excellent site by youth for youth. Another source is Lynne McTaggart's "What Doctors Don't Tell You: The Truth About the Dangers of Modern Medicine."

Because indigos and other sensitive souls are so very sensitive, we can expect that many will be more vulnerable when they consume alcohol or drugs than would other people. One of the aspects is that when they're under the influence of these substances, they are likely to become more impacted by negative energies around them.

Here is a sample of some commonly used drugs and some of their harmful effects:

Ritalin and other similar drugs: These drugs may result in weight loss, exhaustion, paranoia, aggression, panic, and triggering of ongoing psychological problems. Lynne McTaggart reports on a study in which the United Nations found that Ritalin is very often prescribed by physicians without having an assessment done to determine whether the child is actually hyperactive. Long-term use of the drug has also been found to cause irritability and hyperactivity, the very problems the drug is supposed to treat. Ritalin has also been found to suppress growth, makes a child more prone to seizures, and may cause nervousness, anorexia, and toxic psychosis. It has a high potential for addiction. It may also increase suicide risk.

Opioid painkillers: Possible effects include a craving for more painkillers and a decreased interest in sex. It may cause liver toxicity and, being addictive, will cause withdrawal symptoms when stopping use of the drug.

Anti-depressants: Anti-depressants can result in increased anxiety, insomnia, mania, tremors, back pain, digestive and respiratory problems, sexual dysfunction, and increased suicide risk.

Tranquilizers, barbiturates: These are often prescribed to treat anxiety, among other difficulties. Possible long-term effects include chronic tiredness, difficulty sleeping, lack of interest in sex, respiratory difficulties, liver damage, mood swings, and aggression.

Tobacco: Addiction develops very quickly with tobacco and there's a risk of getting mouth and lung cancer, along with other health difficulties, including impotence and heart disease.

Alcohol: Since the symptoms of alcohol are very well known, there's no need to mention them here. Suffice it to say that teens and children can become addicted far more quickly to alcohol than adults can. Tolerance develops very quickly and, as a result, more and more is needed to have the same effect. Damage to the brain, heart, and liver can occur with ongoing use.

Marijuana: Marijuana can cause memory difficulties, attention disorders, and sleep disturbances. It can worsen personality difficulties, such as latent schizophrenia, particularly in young people. It can also negatively impact the higher cognitive functions, such as organization of complex information.

Crack/Cocaine: Cocaine sold on the streets is usually between 3% and 35% pure. When mixed with alcohol, it can increase the euphoric effect of the drug but may result in sudden death. It's highly addictive. Sharing needles can result in the spread of HIV and hepatitis. It can result in loss of cognitive abilities. Many of the homeless people I've done healing work with lived on the streets at least in part because of their addiction to cocaine. Some of them had previously been successful business people and artists.

Ecstasy/MDMA: This drug, which is meant to make people happier for awhile, results in a depletion of the body's natural serotonin, which results in the person feeling less happy than before taking the drug. This effect worsens when taking the drug for a period of time. There's a possibility of a psychological crisis resulting in the need for hospitalization. There's a risk of severe depression. Negative impact increases with greater amounts used.

Psilocybin mushrooms: There is a decrease in serotonin which increases with long-term use, resulting in less happiness overall and an increased risk of depression. Cognitive impairment is also possible. Triggering of underlying mental health difficulties can also occur, such as schizophrenia.

Crystal meth: It can result in permanent damage to the brain's natural neurotransmitter sites in the brain, immune system and metabolism, organ failure, stroke, speeding up of the signs of aging, memory impairment, paranoia, exacerbation of underlying mental problems, and clinical depression.

Given all these symptoms, why not stay clean or use these substances as little as possible? If you're already using them, I recommend you assess whether your sensitivity, creativity, health, relationships, finances, or lifestyle are suffering as a result. Ask the opinion of other people close to you. If you're using one of the legal drugs and want to reduce or quit, do so with the assistance of a physician who is willing to help you do so. If the physician wants to keep you on anti-depressants, for example, consult with two other physicians of your choice.

SECTION III:

EATING DISORDERS, AUTISM, AND SCHIZOPHRENIA

I believe that eating disorders, autism, and schizophrenia occur more frequently among sensitive souls, including indigos, than other people.

Please be aware that I have very little experience with autism or schizophrenia. I'm including some information about these difficulties to assist you, but you must go elsewhere for suggestions regarding holistic healing methods. I'm certain that these issues must be extremely painful. If you suspect that you or your child are carrying negative energies, I recommend you go to the healing methods in the previous sections and try them out.

Eating Disorders

The two main types of eating disorders are anorexia and bulimia. Anorexia is a symptom of our culture because of the glorifying of very slim women in the media. It's related to a woman feeling that she's not good enough as she is. Anorexics are obsessed with losing weight. They may exercise a great deal and they generally eat very little.

In Minuchin's research with families with anorexics, he suggests that anorexia is partly a result of a power struggle between the young woman and her parents. Indigos, who are very sensitive to the issue of power and control, could easily become anorexic if they prefer not to deal directly with feeling controlled, and express it indirectly instead.

Research noted on www.wikipedia.com on this topic states that anorexia lasts an average of 1.7 years. It can be successfully treated in most cases although it can lead to severe physical problems and death if it's allowed to continue. Many anorexics are reluctant to get treatment because it means that they're giving up control. As a result, some need to be hospitalized.

Research found that family therapy using the Maudsley Family Therapy model is successful in resolving this issue in 75% to 90% of cases. Minuchin's family therapy research also showed a high success rate.

As with anorexia, the onset of bulimia is often during adolescence. Many have previously been overweight. They may relapse in adulthood. This is unlike anorexia, in which there's generally no relapse in adulthood. Bulimics can be difficult to detect because they tend to maintain an average weight level, unlike anorexics, who are very thin.

According to the DSM-IV, bulimics are generally obsessed with food, and overeat as a result, followed by major attempts to purge the food. This occurs on many occasions. A small proportion of bulimics don't purge but fast instead or exercise a great deal.

Research discussed in www.wikipedia.com on this topic has found that bulimics tend to come from over-controlling families where there's little nurturing. Research suggests that sexual abuse survivors are more likely to have this disorder.

Research has shown that Maudsley Family Therapy is currently the most useful model to have been extensively researched in the treatment of bulimics.

In my experience, eating disorders are related to self-hatred, depression, negative energies, and shame. They're also highly related to needing to please others while rebelling against control. I recommend using the exercises earlier in this section to assist with those issues.

Story:

I worked with an attractive young woman who wanted to be a model. She wasn't accepted because she didn't have the thin boyish body the industry wanted. She hated herself for having an attractive body that didn't fit the women's magazine look. She became bulimic as a result. She tried to lose weight by throwing up whatever she ate, and came close to starving herself. I worked with her for a few sessions, helping her resolve the negative beliefs and patterns she had picked up from others. I also helped her improve other related issues. She came to have greater self-acceptance and her bulimia was resolved. This is an example of how quickly very serious issues can be resolved with the right approach, even when long-term counseling is believed to be the only solution.

Autism

According to the DSM-IV, the following are required for a person to be considered to be autistic:

I) A total of six or more of the following items:

(A) Qualitative impairments in social interaction, as manifested by at least two of the following:

1. Marked impairments in the use of multiple nonverbal behaviors such as eye-to-eye gaze, facial expression, body posture, and gestures to regulate social interaction;

2. Failure to develop peer relationships appropriate to developmental level;

3. Lack of spontaneous seeking to share enjoyment, interests, or achievements with other people;

4. Lack of social or emotional reciprocity, such as not participating in simple social play or games.

(B) Qualitative impairments in communication as manifested by at least one of the following:

1. Delay in, or total lack of, the development of spoken language (not accompanied by an attempt to compensate through alternative modes of communication such as gesture or mime);

2. In individuals with adequate speech, marked impairment in the ability to initiate or sustain a conversation with others;

3. Stereotyped and repetitive use of language or idiosyncratic language;

4. Lack of varied, spontaneous make-believe play or social imitative play appropriate to their developmental level.

(C) Restricted, repetitive, and stereotyped patterns of behavior, interests, and activities.

(II) Delays or abnormal functioning in at least one of the following areas, with onset prior to age 3 years:

(A) Social interaction;

(B) Language as used in social communication; and/or

(C) Symbolic or imaginative play.

A recent article in a holistic magazine by Brita Belli quoted useful research from various sources, some of which can be found in www.defeatautismnow.com and www.ewg.org. This article said that some children may become autistic as a result of chemicals in their environment. These included mercury, lead, flame retardants, PCBs, and pharmaceutical drugs. The recommendations in the article for parents to avoid the potential damage to their child include the following:

- Minimize your own and your child's exposure to toxins;

- Minimize this exposure especially during pregnancy;

- Minimize exposure to mercury by avoiding eating such fish as shark and swordfish, and limiting exposure to albacore tuna;

- Plastic containers and bath toys can leach chemicals when heated, cleaned, or used for teething;

- Car seats and crib mattresses made with flame retardants; and

- Toys with lead paint.

Pregnant women should take appropriate prenatal vitamins, such as calcium, so that the fetus is not drawing minerals from the mother's bones, where heavy metals are stored.

Some of the literature on indigos states that some crystal children don't bother speaking for the first few years of life. They communicate with their mother psychically and therefore don't bother learning to speak. They may be labeled as autistic as a result.

Psychosis

Psychosis and childhood schizophrenia are major difficulties which need to be assessed by a psychiatrist. These people generally are not in touch with reality a good portion of the time. Psychosis refers to the following:

- Delusions;

- Hallucinations; and

- Difficulty organizing one's thoughts and feelings.

I still remember my professor in my Abnormal Psychology course when I took my bachelor's degree in Psychology saying that the old term "neurotics" refers to people who build castles in the air. On the other hand, he said, psychotics live in them. In other words, psychotics aren't in touch with reality.

According to the DSM-IV, childhood schizophrenia includes the following symptoms:

- Seeing or hearing things that don't exist (hallucinations), especially voices;

- Having beliefs that are not based in reality (delusions);

- Lack of emotion;

- Emotions that are inappropriate to the situation;

- Social withdrawal;

- Poor school performance;

- Decreased ability to practice self-care;

- Strange eating rituals;

- Incoherent speech;

- Illogical thinking; and/or

- Agitation.

Some cases are what are termed catatonic schizophrenics. They barely say anything and may move very little. I discussed two cases that appeared to be catatonics on page 102 of this book. The mothers of both children were certain that their children's difficulties were caused by their getting shots at school when they were very young.

In their discussion of childhood schizophrenia, the Mayo Clinic's website states that it's generally difficult to diagnose these difficulties correctly. When these symptoms begin when a child is young, such as six to eight years old, the symptoms may develop gradually. There may be a sudden onset as well when the individual is older. For more information from the Mayo Clinic on this topic, you can go to http://www. mayoclinic.com/health/paranoid-schizophrenia/DS00862.

These types of difficulties are heart-breaking for the patients and the families. However, when it comes to indigos, who are very sensitive, they can see and feel some things that the rest of us cannot. If they say they hear voices and see strange things, they may be telling the truth. They may be thought of as being schizophrenic when they're actually more aware of these things than the rest of us.

Story:

I recently had a client who was hearing voices and he heard people say negative things to him, although not out loud, when he was in public places and even in his own bedroom. From his perspective, what he was hearing was completely accurate. However, he had a mental breakdown because he consumed a drug many times that is known as magic mushrooms.

He was very sensitive but hadn't learned how to develop a filter so that he wouldn't be bothered by these voices. Think of these voices being like radio waves that we can't see. Almost none of us can see them but they're there. This youth was able to tap into these radio waves from other people. I taught him how to develop a filter, and to send these people love. He had quit using magic mushrooms before seeing me, and I had to help him see that they were part of his difficulties. However, he was still smoking marijuana on a daily basis and this also created difficulties for him. He refused to give that up.

In addition, he also said things that sounded very strange to other people. They especially worried his family and friends, who were concerned that he might have another mental breakdown.

For example, after I did a healing visualization with him, he said that the tree in front of my place was very bright. This sounded a bit crazy. However, what he meant was that he was able to see more clearly and brightly as a result of my assisting him to remove negativity from his mind and his energy field.

I've also seen other youth who went into what appeared to be temporary psychosis as a result of using illegal drugs such as LSD, cocaine, and heroin.

Think of your indigo, if they sound a bit crazy. As I mentioned earlier, indigos can feel and see some things that most other people are unable to relate to. And they're impacted by negative energies from various sources that other people can't feel.

In addition, the dark side of the universe may attack them because of their bright light, and may not attack other people in their environment.

Can anyone relate to your indigo's difficulties? Can a psychic or healer assist them to understand and resolve some of the difficulties before you take them to a psychiatrist?

If they've already seen a psychiatrist and are on medication, you can still assist in resolving the difficulties. However, as I mentioned earlier, you'll never know if there's progress if you don't test it out by taking your child off medication at a pace agreed to by the psychiatrist. You need to remember that some professionals are very married to the medical model and may refuse to take your child off medication. If that occurs, go and see two other specialists.

I recommend that you put your child on anti-psychotic medication only after seeing a number of specialists of various types: naturopaths or homeopaths, healers of various types, psychics, and psychiatrists. I recommend that you put your child on heavy medication very quickly only if they're at moderate to high risk of suicide.

Please contact me if you find holistic healing information that makes use of energy healing so that I may pass it on to other parents.

Individual and family therapy have been found to be helpful with childhood schizophrenia, according to the Mayo Clinic. Please also refer to the research that I mentioned earlier regarding the recovery model with psychosis on page 95 of this book.

SECTION IV:

THE REALLY
TOUGH STUFF:

Transforming Negative Energies
and Blocks
from Sources Inside or Outside
Ourselves

Section IV: The Really Tough Stuff: Transforming   **261**
Negative Energies and Blocks from
Sources Inside or Outside Ourselves

I've personally struggled with many types of darkness in my life and have often become stuck. I was terrified of the dark as a child. I could feel negativity but there was no one there to help me. I lived in what's termed a disengaged family, in which each family member is an isolated island. I kept searching for the best ways of healing these issues over time. I've now worked with over 50 helping professionals and healers of various types. No one really knew how to help me because we didn't realize that I was suffering from difficulties at a variety of levels, including past life issues, DNA, soul group, being impacted by others' suffering, and so on. I and the helpers thought it was all my stuff. It was only through communing more and more fully with Spirit that I learned some methods that helped resolve these issues, along with methods from India and Tibet and other cutting-edge methods from the West.

Part of what I learned is that there are really no enemies. Whatever negative energy impacts me is really a friend in disguise, even if that's not their intention. It may be people or dark energies that attack us to protect their turf, to steal our money, or whatever. The bottom line is that there are no coincidences. Difficulties that occur to us happen for a reason. Negativity is intended by the universe to push us to grow, to go more and more fully toward the light, to surrender our pettiness, and to serve more fully. The more we struggle against this, the more painful the lesson becomes until we finally get it.

In my experience, traditional forms of helping and healing aren't sufficient for indigos and other sensitive souls.

Unfortunately, a great many end up on medication because they see their situations as hopeless, and the professionals who prescribe the medications see this as the only solution.

Before I discuss how to deal with dark energies, I will quote Lady Nada, channeled by a young indigo. This shows you that when you become very sensitive, it doesn't necessarily mean that you are mentally disturbed or being attacked by negative energies when you feel bad. In fact, our sensitivity, although it can be very difficult to handle, is actually a great gift that pushes us to gain more and more mastery over our lives:

"I comprehend that as you become more sensitive to the light and energy around you, you also become more aware of your own negative thought habits, beliefs, or actions. You will become sensitive to the touch of any kind of negative energy that may seep into your reality through another person or your actions. It is unfortunately a part of mastering your being. As you grow spiritually anchoring greater light into your being you may find that the smallest things, comments or situations in your life can affect you in a negative way such as irritation or annoyance, because you have become extremely sensitive to energy vibrations. By protecting yourself and focusing on the core love of the Creator this can be combated. There is a need for constant cleansing to reduce any effects of negativity, whether it stems from outside influences or swells from within your being as fear and doubt. Cleansing and healing are the keys to spiritual growth. As you peel away layers of energy you reveal the divine jewel and star of light that inhabits the physical body (http://goddesslight.wordpress.com/2008/07/09/message-from-lady-nada/).

Chapter 20
Negative Energies

There are eight types of issues that I believe must be considered when indigos and other sensitive souls experience difficulties, beyond psychotherapy's usual focus on mind, emotions, body, and relationships:

- Secondary trauma;

- Historical trauma;

- Soul and soul group issues;

- Past lives and parallel lives;

- Negative thought forms;

- Curses;

- Entities; and

- Negative energies of various types – in the individual, the home, or the land.

These are essential for us to consider with all the difficulties experienced by indigos and other sensitive souls. In addition, as I discussed earlier, these souls are more sensitive to other forms of negativity as well, such as power lines, bleached flour, red dye, and so on. One may also have an insufficiency of energy flow as a result of blockage, or too much energy coming in as a result of being too open. These must be regulated and balanced. I will only discuss the factors that have not been discussed elsewhere in this book. Remember that none of these dark energies are negative, although we tend to see them that way. They're all an opportunity for us to grow more and more fully.

Past Lives and Parallel Lives

Reincarnation is so commonly discussed in the West in the past few decades that it needs no introduction here. Whenever an individual is struggling with a personal issue or with someone else, it's always important to consider past life issues. I mention past life issues in some of my case examples throughout this book.

Some believe they don't deserve much due to past life experiences, and they greatly limit their capacity as a result.

When we resolve past life difficulties, we need to do so at the seat of the soul or higher self, which is six inches (15 centimeters) above our heads. It's also important to resolve these issues at the causal body, which is like the suitcase of the soul, which carries both our positive and negative karma. This is at a higher dimension. Although you quite often need to know the precise issue that needs to be transformed, this is not always necessary. As a general rule, try asking your higher self or God to resolve any negativity from past lives that is part of the difficulty. If this doesn't work, consider obtaining training to learn how to very precisely assess and transform these issues or see a healer who can do this. I believe, as others do, that our difficulties are negative karma that we're working through or lessons that our soul needs to learn. Hence, past life issues are always involved in one way or another.

Negative Thought Forms

Negative thought forms occur when someone is upset with us. Most of us aren't sensitive enough to feel these energies, although some are very deeply affected by this. For example, a person's anger, whether they express it or not, creates a dark cloud over your head and blocks the light from coming in, as with a cloud blocking the sunlight. This is very simple to transform from darkness to light when you can identify the cause and you know how to do the cleansing.

Think of U.S. President Bill Clinton. A great many people were angry with him. A big part of that was that he sabotaged himself in a variety of ways, including his own personal transgressions. Many of us sabotage our growth because we have dark energies that limit us or because we have beliefs that we don't deserve more. One of the options we have for limiting our growth is to get people upset with us. This results in negative thought forms over our heads, which block the light from coming in.

As another example, a whole clan may attack an individual. One case of this is a couple I know who fell in love while each was married to someone else. They separated from their spouses and moved in together. Their children and many others were outraged and sent them a great deal of negativity and curses. I did a variety of things to help resolve these issues between the couple and the clan, and one of the aspects was to transform from darkness to light the negative thought forms from the clan, using the following exercise.

In terms of indigos, think of your indigo, who acts out towards others and speaks his truth, and is disliked for it. Because of this, it's very easy for indigos to have a great deal of negative energy thrown at them.

Exercise:

Have light come in from above and have it go to the first six inches (15 centimeters) over your head. Imagine the light cleansing away the negativity from there in the same way as the sun dissipates early morning fog.

Curses

Curses can be much more difficult and complex to resolve than negative thought forms. With the latter, the person is unaware that they are causing us harm – they're simply upset toward us. With ritualized curses, they harm us intentionally. It's similar to voodoo, although some people who have sufficient spiritual power can cause us great harm by having negative thoughts toward us.

I'll give you an example and a brief exercise, although you may need more than this to fully resolve a curse.

<u>**Story:**</u>

To give you a personal example, I was working with a First Nations client who had been in a car accident. His girlfriend, with him in the car, was killed because he was very drunk and crashed into a cliff. His lawyer advised him to work with a therapist and attend a substance abuse treatment center before the matter was dealt with in court, as a way of trying to reduce the penalty. This client booked sessions with me but refused to do any healing work with me. He just sat there and didn't want to talk with me. He simply wanted to be able to say that he had spent time with a therapist.

He also asked me to refer him to a substance abuse treatment center. I did so, against my better judgment, because that is not something I usually do. I agreed to do this in the hope that he'd then be willing to work with me. I wrote a brief note in the application form stating that there was a legal matter involved, so that the staff would hopefully assist him with this issue. My client was very angry with me for revealing this. As a result, he and his family cursed me, using chanting, drums, and other methods. I was not aware of any of this at the time. However, my life stopped completely. For example, right after they cursed me, I had a full day of clients booked – not one of them showed up and only one called to cancel. I had a number of checks expected to arrive in the mail, and they were all delayed for a long period of time. I also lost the contract at the

Indian Reservation because this client complained about me. My practice became stagnant and no new clients were coming in.

I still had no idea what was going on. I spoke with three psychics and they told me that I had been cursed and by whom. I hadn't believed this to be possible before then. I thought that if you don't believe in curses they can't affect you. Wrong!

I worked with a number of healers and psychics to help me resolve this block but nothing worked. After a while, a friend found an eagle feather with a bear claw tied to it in the water of Griffin Lake in British Columbia. He gave it to me, thinking it was meant for me but not understanding what it was for. A couple of weeks later, the same friend was in the southern United States and picked up a hitchhiker from Mexico. They discussed various things, but did not talk about me and my Indian curse. As he was getting out of the car, the hitchhiker gave my friend a stone and told him that it was to ward off curses. My friend then thought it was meant for me from Spirit and he gave it to me the next time I saw him.

The feather with the bear claw and the stone were clearly brought to me by Spirit to help resolve my curses. I had been praying and asking Spirit for help, all without apparent success. As a result of this darkness, more and more negativity was attracted to me because my life was in shambles. As a Hermetic law of the universe states – like attracts

> like. So the darkness I carried and the despair I felt resulted in more negativity coming to me. And then, no coincidence whatsoever, Spirit brought me these items to transform the native curses so that my life and my practice could move forward again.

Sometimes, we can ask for help for years and remain stuck. In my case, fortunately, my prayers were answered fairly quickly. I learned from this and other incidents how to determine if a client has a curse, as well as how to transform various types of curses, including curses against our clan, against our being prosperous, against us from past lives, powerful curses from aboriginal people and others, and so on.

An example of this type of negativity is the statement from the Old Testament that the sins of the fathers will be visited upon their sons. You need to know that you have a curse and where it's from, for you to be able to transform it. Otherwise, all your best efforts will fail. Very sensitive people, including indigos, can be greatly affected by these types of issues, whereas others seem to be completely unaffected.

Another example from my life is that when I was preparing to go do some healing work in Haiti following the earthquake, I sent positive healing energy there to help resolve some of the negativity. As a result, I ended up receiving curses from voodoo because its practitioners don't want things to improve. This was very useful for me because it gave me an opportunity to practice healing voodoo-related issues before I actually went there. Because of this, I was better prepared than I otherwise would have been. If we look at things correctly, everything is actually positive and useful for our growth.

It can also be very useful to use positive spiritual energies from the same source as the curse. In my case, I asked Great Spirit to help me transform the curse from the aboriginal client with the help of the eagle feather with the bear claw and the stone, as well as the First Nations ancestors. With the voodoo curse, I used local energies from Haiti, asking the positive side of voodoo to assist me in resolving the curse. I also asked for help from Christ energy because many people in Haiti combine Catholicism with voodoo.

If you think there is a ritualized curse against you, your family, your business, your group, or your child, some psychics may be able to help you, but others will not. Most psychics can see some things that others can't, but in my experience, most don't have the skills to help to resolve curses or transform negative energies. If you remain stuck with this or other difficult energies, feel free to contact us and we'll help you determine the causes of the blocks and resolve them.

Discarnates

There are two main types of entities. The first are discarnate souls.

Some years ago, I decided to do some spiritual exercises in a cemetery in order to resolve the fear of dying that we all carry, although most of us are unconscious of it. I also went there to work toward increasing my compassion for all beings. This exercise stems from both Hinduism and Buddhism. I thought I was doing wonderfully well in the cemetery. I shed some tears, opening my heart more and more to the suffering of people who had died, and practiced giving everyone who had died or been left behind compassion for their suffering.

In the next couple of weeks, however, I connected with three separate psychic friends who didn't know each other. Each told me that I had picked up entities. They helped me resolve the issue because I knew nothing about this at the time, and told me not to go to the cemetery again. Of course, I did because it was so wonderful for my spiritual development. When I met with my friends again, they gave me a tongue-lashing for going again – and they helped me to resolve the issue again. I went through the same process a third time, picking up entities again, before deciding that I'd grown enough in the cemetery. Wonderful growth – it was very worthwhile for me. In the process and in my later work, I learned how to resolve various types of issues relating to discarnate entities.

We can pick up a variety of negative energies in a cemetery so please don't do what I did, do what I say – stay away from there unless you have a strong support group that will be able to help you to resolve the negativity that you'll pick up in the cemetery.

In my experience, about 80% of discarnates/ghosts are very simple to transform, once you know how. The other 20% will require more, using other approaches. To cleanse yourself of most of these entities, I recommend that you find out how many entities you are carrying. Then you ask that they be released by saying: "I ask the low part of the soul to reconnect with the highest part and not to trouble anyone again." If this doesn't work, they may have a message for you, and you need to hear that before they are prepared to leave. Other types of issues may also be involved before the discarnate is ready to leave.

Dark Energies

The other type of entity is energy from the dark side of the universe that attempts to block our light. They are particularly drawn to people who have a great deal of light in them, such as indigos, light workers, and other sensitive souls, as a way of trying to block our light.

However, if we think negatively, we'll attract those kinds of energies to us even if our thoughts or emotions are unconscious. People who abuse alcohol or drugs also attract negative energies to them.

To quote David Hawkins, an enlightened psychiatrist and one of my favorite writers, from his book, "I: Reality and Subjectivity": "As one evolves, one is, as the Buddha says, beset by demons of all sorts as well as by psychic attacks. And they do indeed manifest, sometimes directly in a worldly form and setting." He mentioned that both Christ and the Buddha discussed these issues. Hawkins spoke of three types of negative energies:

1.   Satanic forces, personified as Mara by Buddha. These dark energies try to entice us through such things as "sin," violent movies and video games,

drugs, and other activities that serve to lower our vibration and to lose touch with the light;

2. Demonic forces are usually in a particular person, such as in a serial killer, who might say that they didn't mean to kill, but they were asked to do it by what they perceived to be God; and

3. Luciferic forces, which are more subtle and have to do with such issues as power and fame. They try to seduce us as they did with Jesus, offering him the kingdom.

Hawkins discusses that we need to avoid these energies. They are fairly obvious to detect in his view because, as he puts it, they're very stupid. Their messages are obviously meant to seduce us and get us off track.

Joshua David Stone, another of my favorite writers, says the following regarding this issue: "Light workers are often under attack from the Dark Brotherhood, also known as the Black Lodge. They are not to be feared as long as you have the tools to remain in self-mastery."

Indigos and other sensitive souls are more at risk with these dark energies than most other people because of the amount of light they carry. It's true that we attract darkness to ourselves, but it's also true that as we focus more and more on the light, darkness tries to stop our progress more and more. People can often shame us by telling us that we create our own reality, and so we attract negativity to ourselves by the negativity we carry. That may be true. However, many people who say these things can't relate to some of these negative energies because they're not sufficiently advanced yet. We can believe that we create/manifest our own reality. Although there's a great deal of truth to this, I find it a bit too simplistic.

Remember Jesus. Remember Aristotle who was forced to drink a cup of poisonous hemlock because he spoke truth. Remember the saints who were tortured. Remember Tibetan Buddhist monks, whose monasteries have been destroyed and many of whom have been tortured until this day. Dark forces attacking the light. And yet these are all opportunities for us to grow more fully. The universe is designed that way to help us keep growing and transcending.

Despite the negativity experienced in Tibet, the Dalai Lama still advises us to give our enemies compassion. We, as budding bodhisattvas taking steps to heal the sorrow of other beings and make the world a better place, need to give everyone caring and tenderness, no matter how they treat us. Thank God no one gets tortured for their spiritual work in the Western world. It's easier for us to do this than for a Tibetan Buddhist monk being tortured. Of course, we need to be in our power and set limits when people abuse us. This is one of the aspects of mastery.

And I fully agree with Deepak Chopra's perspective that all these dark forces are not to be feared because they're all facets of God. And therefore all of it is to be loved. These dark forces are wonderful for pushing us toward growth, toward the Godhead. This perspective helps us to go out of the world of polarities and into a state of unconditional love and greater peace.

Exercise:

Ask Krishna or Kali to transform all entities from the dark side of the universe that you carry. Ask that it be done immediately. You can choose to ask other beings for help as well. Christ may work best for most Christians. However, in many experiments working with these issues, I've found Krishna and Kali to be the most effective.

I've provided you with many of the tools to gain self-mastery in this book. You simply need to practice them and then consult with a wise guide when you get stuck. And go further. And then you'll get stuck again. And you search again. And then you go further. The spiritual path, as many have said, is always three steps forward, and two steps back, and four steps forward, and two back.

Just remember, all darkness is also part of God. Everything that happens to us is part of our journey, part of our lessons, as we grow toward greater and greater light. And as David Hawkins has said, we can only go as high as we've been low.

Negative Energy in our Home and on the Land

There may be some very negative energies in our home or in the building in which we live, as well as on the land that our home is on. There may be discarnates, death energy, curses, and other forms of negativity, as well as negativity from our neighbors and adjoining properties. These all need to be transformed. You've now learned how to handle all of these. You simply need to practice now. It's quite okay if you get stuck. That's part of our journey and of our learning.

The following story is an example of negative energy in the home.

Story:

One of my early indigo clients was a 13-year-old who did terrible things. She stole the family car several times and crashed it twice. She ran away from home. One day, her parents asked her to move to a different bedroom in another part of the house. She flatly refused. When her parents pressed her about this, she told them that she had been blocking what she called a porthole to the dark side of the universe – she was keeping her finger in a hole in the dike, so to speak, so that the family home wouldn't get flooded by negativity.

The daughter had been sacrificing herself for her family to protect them from the darkness, although she was being severely impacted and acted out some of it.

Among other methods used in the healing, I gave the family a "hand" to close the porthole energetically.

I've worked with negative energy on properties and on the land in a wide variety of ways. For example, a client experiences difficulty in their home because the neighbor's energy is negative. The neighbor might be depressed or the couple could be in conflict. In one case, my client's neighbor was a funeral director and his negative energy greatly impacted my client. In other cases, houses were built on sacred native land. In others, many First Nations people had died when the Europeans came. All of these energies can greatly impact indigos and other sensitive souls without their having the least idea as to what's causing them grief. All of these are easy to resolve once you find out what the causes are and know how to resolve them, as I've shown you in this book.

Chapter 21
When Nothing Else Works

There are situations where we try everything and nothing works, no matter what. One of the causes of this is what is termed defense mechanisms – unconscious mechanisms for self-protection, which we discussed earlier on page 117. We're often not aware of them in ourselves, although other people may be able to clearly see them. For example, our indigos can see right through our various forms of hiding and avoiding and are usually quite willing to point these things out to us. Following are some of the defenses we can exhibit – denial, repression, regression, avoidance, rationalization, projection, reaction formation, introjection, somatization, and turning against the self:

- **Denial:** Not admitting to ourselves or others that we have a particular problem, such as denying that we're angry or have a substance abuse problem;

- **Repression:** We suppress our emotions, such as anger, because we think it's bad to feel that way.

Many women suppress their anger, and many men suppress most emotions other than anger;

- **Regression:** When under stress, we act as though we're much younger than our age. For example, when very upset or sick, a 12-year-old might whine like a small child;

- **Avoidance:** This refers to, for example, living "in our heads" as a way of avoiding feeling painful emotions;

- **Rationalization:** Making excuses – explaining things away rather than looking at ourselves;

- **Projection:** Denying that we have a particular emotion and seeing it in others instead. For example, rather than admitting that we have anger, we instead see others as being angry;

- **Reaction formation:** Replacing one feeling with another, such as becoming angry and aggressive when we're actually afraid;

- **Introjection:** Identifying with another, as with an aggressor, i.e., a child becoming like their aggressive parent;

- **Somatization:** Shutting down our feelings to the point where they affect our body through illness instead; and

- **Turning against the self:** This refers to having a negative feeling toward someone, such as anger. We then turn this negative feeling toward ourselves instead. For example, the anger we feel toward someone is suppressed and turns into anger toward ourselves or into depression.

These are important for you to be aware of, because they can play havoc with your life. Your indigo will be happy to point out your defenses and avoidance to you. However, they will also have defenses just as the rest of us do, but their acting them out may be more intense than with others. For example, if an indigo suppresses their anger and their power, they might become very depressed or even suicidal.

These defenses block our growth. For this reason, it's important to discover our own defenses and resolve them if we're to move forward more effectively toward what we want. We resolve them partly through being aware of what we do to avoid our pain. Also, ask someone who's prepared to be honest with you about your defenses. You can then gradually work toward changing your behavior. This is easier said than done, however, but absolutely worth the effort. We all need to help each other with our blocks, so that we can live healthier, happier, and more productive lives.

With someone who is not prepared to deal with their defenses, such as an alcoholic parent, regularly confronting them with their imperfections will only make things worse. It's far better to use the solution-focused approach discussed earlier in this book on page 116, in which the goal is to focus on when things were more positive instead, and build on that. The questions to focus on, as I mentioned earlier, are:

- What were you doing when the situation was a bit better?

- When did this happened most recently?

- What were you doing differently at those times?

- Do more of what you were doing when the problem was not happening.

If we're unable to think of exceptions when the problem is absent, then the goal is to just experiment and do something different and see what happens. Focus on the positives until the situation changes, and then continue with the positive focus.

The third approach to dealing with serious blocks is what has been termed reverse polarity popularized through EFT – Emotional Freedom Technique. This was developed by Roger Callaghan in TFT – Thought Field Therapy.

From this perspective, our blocks are generally unresolved beliefs, hidden from our view. This disrupts our energy field. We must transform them before we can move forward.

When our electromagnetic field is disrupted, EFT and other healing methods don't work or the benefits will only last a short time. People in this state don't respond well to energy work overall, or to life in general. It's as though the batteries have been inserted incorrectly in a flashlight. People who have this condition feel undeserving at a deep level. As a result of such negative beliefs about themselves and the world, people make the same self-limiting mistakes over and over again.

Some people's polarities are reversed in one or two areas only, such as with difficulty resolving an addiction. If the reversed polarity is chronic, it's called neurological disorganization. If that's the case for you or your child, do the belly button correction described below many times a day every day to retrain your body's energy system. This will help you develop a more positive outlook on life. Others may only need to use this technique once.

Reversed polarity can occur as a result of a major stress, such as divorce, death of a loved one, or a major move. For others, it's a result of poor lifestyle – eating poorly, not enough sleep, working too hard. It's reported that smoking cigarettes can also cause this. Allergies can also be the cause, or long-term stress. Your system simply shuts down. Clinical research has shown that these conditions are often associated with the following symptoms: depression, exhaustion not linked to a physical imbalance, poor memory, anxiety, fear, feelings of hopelessness, dizziness, immune system disturbances, poor coordination, headaches, dissociation, reversing words or letters as in saying left instead of right, or reversing letters when you're typing. Other symptoms related to reversed polarity are chronic fatigue syndrome, muscular pains, hormonal disturbances, autoimmune deficiencies, or cancer.

Some people may have made a decision to shut down in childhood because of unmet needs. They've simply turned off from life, expecting little from it. Life then confirms their expectations because they're not open to receiving.

To resolve this condition, you need to sleep well, avoid substances to which you react badly, and eat well. The following exercises will also help.

Exercise:

To resolve simpler cases of psychological reversal, rub the neurolymphatic reflex, a point one inch above the physical heart. Rub it for about ten seconds. If the condition is not resolved or is chronic, do the following exercise.

Belly Button Correction:

Put three fingers in your belly button and hold there, while doing the following:

a. Rub under your nose;

b. Rub your lower lip at the middle point;

c. Massage both collar bone points; and

d. Rub coccyx (bottom of tail bone).

PART III:

THE
FAMILY

The topic of indigo children, other sensitive souls, and the family is very complex. There are many factors to take into consideration, including family composition, cultural issues, the number of indigos in the family, dysfunctional issues such as substance abuse and delinquency, and parent-teen conflict. And there are also the soul and soul group issues, as well as interactions with larger systems such as schools, physicians, etc. While professional and holistic books on indigos as well as on psychotherapy and healing contain many good ideas, there is no literature that explores all these issues in depth.

My forthcoming book will cover the full range of issues that affect indigos and sensitive souls and their families, which we may call "indigo families."

Chapter 1
The Gifts of Having an Indigo or Other Very Sensitive Child

To start with, I'll briefly mention some of the gifts of having an indigo or a sensitive child in your family. There are many more – add your own.

Being involved with indigos forces many of us as their parents, teachers, and helpers to grow and become more open and honest, to know our minds and express them, and to have clear boundaries and be prepared to say "no" or "yes." We also need to be in a place of integrity and in touch with our higher, wiser side much of the time. In other words, although most indigos don't come from the same soul group as their parents, they're here to help us and other adults to grow beyond our comfort zone. It just makes things worse for them and for us if we refuse to hear them and resist their attempt to create a better home, a better school, and a better world. And here is more for you to consider:

- You need to be more sensitive to deal with them;

- Provide a stronger setting to help them express their gifts;

- Be more connected to your heart and spirit;

- Develop more compassion for your child's imperfections;

- You need to be very straight and clear in your communication;

- Practice authoritative parenting – a combination of love and strength;

- You need to look after yourself more;

- Work more fully as a team with your spouse and other family members;

- You can't be either authoritarian or laissez faire (too laid back) with your child;

- Develop more compassion for your imperfections, and ask your child to give you compassion too – you're learning as well;

- You need a stronger support network for you and your child;

- You need to explain your child's needs to others;

- Stand up for their needs and rights more with other authority figures; and

- You need to have understanding and supportive friends, a support team, such as a supportive teacher and school principal, a psychologist or therapist with a holistic orientation, child minders, and perhaps a naturopath or physician who is unlikely to prescribe medication when there are other alternatives and understanding friends. It really takes a village to raise an indigo.

There are many more. Build a list with other people.

Another aspect that I'll briefly mention here is the country that indigos live in. Think of indigo children being born in very patriarchal cultures where the child, especially a girl, is not supposed to have a voice. Think of an indigo being born in a country that's at war. The indigos are being born there in the hope of helping to change those parts of the world. It'll be fascinating to see how this turns out. We can be sure that many of them will be mistreated and reviled. Some will likely need help in their efforts to make their area a better part of the world.

Chapter 2
Bonding

As I discuss bonding issues, I'd like you to think not only of your child, but also yourself, and others you're closely involved with. Far more people have difficulties in bonding than you might suspect. These difficulties can generally be healed fairly quickly. I've used a variety of methods to do this over time, and I've found the methods in the previous section to be very helpful for this.

In this section, I'll discuss one of the more important issues for children and families – bonding. Bonding difficulties are one of the most profound factors affecting children and youth. Because they're so sensitive, indigos and other sensitive souls tend to be more deeply affected by bonding difficulties. Although this tends to affect everyone, no matter what their soul age, I believe that bonding difficulties affect indigos and other sensitive souls even more. This is true either through increased anger, weaker relationship between parent and child, not wanting to take responsibility for one's life, withdrawal, physical sensitivity to foods, ADHD, or illness. If bonding difficulties are not addressed, the consequences can be traumatic and damaging to parents, the indigo children, siblings, and others.

The Family Life Cycle

As the family therapy literature shows, there are a number of stages in the family life cycle. If you wish to read more on this topic, I recommend "The Expanded Family Life Cycle" by Betty Carter and Monica McGoldrick.

The stages of the family life cycle are as follows. Please note that these vary depending on the family and on one's cultural background:

- The launching of the single young adult;

- Bonding of the young couple;

- The joining of families through a common law relationship or marriage;

- Family with young children;

- Family with adolescents;

- Launching the children and empty nest; and

- The family in later life.

In this section, we'll explore the bonding issue as it relates to the family with children. Our ability to bond in a healthy way with our mate depends on whether we were able to create a healthy bond with our parents, developing healthy trust, an open heart, and other qualities. Of course, it also depends on whether we did the healing work that we needed to help resolve issues from our past, including childhood and past lives.

Couples need to be able to discuss concerns, give each other support and compassion, and help each other when appropriate, both as a couple and as parents. If we don't do this well, our indigos will add to the difficulties. The stress created by them can all too easily result in our becoming stressed and reactive, and increase the size of the imperfections in our personality as well as in our relationship with our mate. For example, if we have low self-esteem, interacting with our indigo can easily increase it. Or if we get stressed easily, our indigo will often increase that. If we don't communicate well with our spouse, this can result in major difficulties with our indigos.

After going through the bonding stage successfully, the couple is in a good position for the next phase – having a child. In this stage, a number of tasks need to be accomplished. The mother must be well-bonded with the baby; the father must accommodate and support this new relationship between mother and child; and the couple must find new and different ways of connecting with each other. Bonding between mother and child begins during the pregnancy. The father's support of the mother needs to increase during that time because of her increased vulnerability.

Modern fathers begin to bond with the baby when very small, including through direct child care, unlike most fathers 20 or 30 years ago and earlier. Most fathers need to grow beyond the role models they know from their childhood if they want to be excellent parents. The couple also needs to have healthy connections with their extended network. This varies a great deal depending on the cultural background.

The roles of parents will change as the child grows up, presenting different challenges to parents over time. As you know, parents need to act differently with a one-year-old compared to a child starting school, or a teenager.

There's no such thing as perfect bonding, because none of us is perfect and there are many factors outside our control that can impact the bonding between us and our child. The reality is that we all have many things to learn and we're all imperfect, even when we do our best. We need to accept our imperfections and work on resolving them as best we can, while acknowledging that there will always be room for growth. Our children are our teachers and our indigos even more so.

If we blame ourselves or somebody else for challenges, deny the situation, or see things as being worse than they actually are, it adds to the difficulties. Better to look at ourselves straight on and admit to our imperfections and the mistakes we may have made, and then take steps to resolve them. The same applies to our partner's difficulties. When we're well bonded with them, most indigos are very forgiving if we acknowledge our errors and weaknesses and apologize for them when appropriate.

When I speak of mother and baby in this section, I'm doing so for the sake of convenience. Think of it as the relationship with the primary caretaker, including the relationship with the father if he's also very involved in parenting.

Positive Bonding

As research by Daniel Siegel, one of the most important writers in the field of neurology and relationships, and others has shown, the degree of our ability to connect positively with people is directly related to our relationship with our primary caretaker. According to this research, the most important period for this is the first year and a half of the child's life. Daniel Goleman, an eminent psychologist who has developed the concepts of emotional and social intelligence, has also summarized much of the research on bonding in "Social Intelligence." Other useful books on this topic include "Hold on to Your Kids" by Gordon Neufeld and Gabor Maté, "Connected Parenting" by Jennifer Kolari, and "Attachment, Trauma, and Healing" by Terry Levy and Michael Orlans.

Positive bonding occurs through the interaction between the mother and baby. For example, she smiles at the baby, and the baby then smiles back. Or the baby smiles at the mother and she smiles back. The baby will shut down temporarily if the mother doesn't respond because her attention is elsewhere or if she's under stress.

A mother who is emotionally available to her child also usually resolves her baby's concerns fairly quickly when they cry. If the baby is upset, she nurtures and meets the baby's needs quickly most of the time.

These brief conversations between mother and baby, based totally on emotions, form the foundation of your relationship with your child. It will later form the foundation of all our adult relationships. Emotion and bonding are at the core of every communication we have with people. As the child develops a strong bonding relationship with the mother, the child is then able to bond more fully with the father, siblings, and other people.

Bonding and healthy child care have a profound impact on the baby's brain development. Consistently dealing with the baby's upsets results in fewer stress hormones in the baby. It also results in a fuller development of the hippocampus, a part of the midbrain which assists in resolving stress and trauma. As a result, the baby gradually develops the ability to remain emotionally stable over the course of its life. Think of this in comparison to the recommendations of Dr. Spock, the famous physician from a few decades ago who guided a generation of parents. His recommendations included feeding a baby on a schedule, and leaving the baby to cry the rest of the time.

The baby reacts to the mother not being emotionally available first by protesting and, if this doesn't work, by turning away. If the mother doesn't respond positively a fair proportion of the time, this results in the baby becoming overly dependent. Rather than a small child developing the confidence to go out and explore a bit when they're able to crawl and then walk, they become clingy. The baby will end up expecting that their needs will not be met much of the time. If this happens often enough, it will negatively affect the bonding between the mother and baby.

Donald Winnicott, one of the writers from object relations theory, which focuses on the early mother-child relationship, coined the term "good enough mothering." This means that the baby will become a healthy adult if their mother responds to their needs at least 70% of the time and adapts appropriately to the child at the different stages of infancy. For example, when the baby is very small, they require a great deal of nurturing. As the child becomes a toddler, they require more freedom to move and explore.

The mother's appropriate responses to the child's changing needs gives the baby a sense of control as well as healthy bonding to the mother. In the process, the mother needs to respond positively to the infant's frustrations. If this doesn't proceed in a healthy way, the infant develops what Winnicott called a "false self" rather than a "true self." An individual with a false self will have difficulty creating healthy connections with others.

Research in the new field of neurobiology of interpersonal experience confirms some of the earlier clinical research on bonding. Daniel Siegel's recent research has shown that if the baby experiences a degree of stress that is not too overwhelming, its brain will develop a stronger ability to be resilient to stress over time than that of a child who is highly protected from stress. In other words, a mother who works very hard to always keep her baby satisfied is not doing her child any favors.

On the other hand, research with rats has shown that baby rats who are highly nurtured will grow up to be more resilient and handle stress more easily, whereas those with less nurturing will handle it less well. It's a question of degree – a great deal of nurturing is very healthy for the child, although excessive nurturing is not.

Recent research by Cassidy and Shaver has shown that 55% of people have the ability to be in a healthy relationship. Their bonding was mostly secure or they had healed unresolved bonding difficulties. Twenty percent have what is termed "anxious bonding," such as insecurity, jealousy, and a sense of unworthiness. Their parents were not emotionally available much of the time. Twenty-five percent of people are more closed from shutting down as small children as a result of their primary parent being emotionally unavailable much of the time. Our orientation in terms of bonding can change over time, depending on whether we have positive or negative relationships as adults and how we integrate these later experiences.

Because indigos are very sensitive, strong-minded, and independent, we may wonder if our child has difficulties in bonding or personality problems. Although either of those may be valid, the reality is that the differences may simply be a result of who they are as a soul. If you have uncertainties about which of these three applies to your child, I recommend that you learn to use, or work with someone who knows, applied kinesiology/muscle testing or the use of a pendulum to help you assess these issues. If you test yourself, just be aware that you may get false readings because of your unconscious beliefs. This can also occur if you test someone close to you, such as your spouse or a close friend.

As you'll realize, this and other research from the West doesn't take into account bonding-related issues at the soul and soul group levels.

Difficulties in Bonding

If we had difficulty bonding as children, it may be difficult for us to communicate and interact well with others as adults. As John Lennon sang to us, "One thing you can't hide is when you're crippled inside." Unless these issues are healed, it's likely to affect our relationship with our children as well, and even more so with our very sensitive indigo child. One aspect of this is that because they're so sensitive, they can sense when we're not fully present more easily than another child can, and they will react accordingly.

When a mother is unavailable much of the time, the baby may experience this as abandonment, and may interpret this as not being lovable. Unless this is healed, the child could feel this way their entire life, and act accordingly.

This applies even before the baby is born. The baby feels very intensely what's going on with the mother because she's the baby's home. The baby is greatly affected through the mother by what's going on around her – her relationship with her partner, her fear of not having enough money, her discomfort with being pregnant, the pain she experiences during delivery, moving from one residence to another during pregnancy, intense political upheaval, and so on. The baby takes the mother's suffering, stress, and worries as its own, and these will impact the child later on. It's likely to be even more so with indigos and other sensitive children.

At birth, the baby's connection with their spirit is very strong, and this results in the negativity that it carries not being sufficient to block its connection with its spirit. And so the baby comes out with eyes shining brightly, full of spirit. However, these various difficulties have an impact in diminishing the child's access to light as they get older. Those who are less well-bonded with their mother will be more impacted by their own negativity and that around them over time. They're more likely to become easily upset or angry, or be easily traumatized.

The most likely time for these to be acted out is during adolescence, when so many changes are happening to youth in terms of hormones, social context, and physical growth. Depending on the degree of bonding difficulty, these difficulties may affect them earlier in childhood or when they have intimate relationships as adults, for example. These factors apply to everyone but again, they're amplified with sensitive souls in general, and even more so with indigos.

Babies don't have the ability to understand that their mother is preoccupied by a variety of difficulties on an ongoing basis. They take the disconnection personally. The result is reduced trust toward the parent, and likely toward all adults, as well as toward life in general. The baby can also end up feeling unlovable. The impact of the infant's withdrawing is permanent, affecting a number of areas – including the brain, social development, and giving up too easily when hurdles arise in life. Different people are affected in different ways.

The good news is that these issues can be healed deeply and fairly quickly if worked on in the right way. Exercises in this book can help you to do so. Some healers will have the ability to assist you to heal some of these issues quickly as well. As I've said elsewhere, I strongly recommend that you stay with a helper or healer no more than three sessions if you don't feel better or see any progress, no matter how warm or confident they are that they can help you over time.

Bonding between mother and baby can be affected by the factors noted in the list in the exercise that follows, among others. Notice in that list that many of these have nothing to do with the parents' behavior directly but are related to broader factors, such as employment, soul-related issues, health, death of a loved one, etc.

The following is meant as information, not as an opportunity for you to beat yourself up for being imperfect or for your child having difficulties. All of us have things to learn as human beings and as parents, and this is an opportunity to see ourselves and our child more clearly. When we see imperfections in ourselves, it's an opportunity to give ourselves caring and tenderness, and to focus on healing our wounds – not beat ourselves up. The same applies with our loved ones.

My experience and recent work on couples therapy has shown that the bonding difficulties of one spouse in childhood can be healed to a great extent by having a supportive and nurturing partner. If you're interested in this, you can refer to books by Sue Johnson and Brent Atkinson for methods on assisting couples to heal old bonding difficulties. Atkinson's book is for helping professionals. I also recommend "Embracing the Beloved: Relationship as a Path of Awakening" by Stephen and Ondrea Levine.

As I've mentioned, because they're so sensitive, bonding difficulties can impact indigos and other sensitive souls more than other people. On the one hand, people can become more hyper-sensitive specifically as a result of bonding difficulties. On the other hand, some children whose families experience major difficulties also become more resilient.

Even if we were imperfect as parents in the past, we can take steps to assist in healing the bonding wounds of our children as well. Remember, we and our children contracted at the soul level to be together because we all had things to learn from it.

Exercise:

The following are some of the potential causes of bonding difficulties. Be aware that there will not necessarily be bonding difficulties if one or more of these issues are at play for you or your child. However, if you or your child has bonding difficulties, knowing the causes will make it far easier for you to heal them.

Please checkmark the factors that fit for you. They're listed in a time sequence. Then you can do some healing work on them for yourself using the exercises from the previous section. After that, I recommend you either do it for your child, or assist your child to do the exercise if they're old enough and willing to participate.

☐ *Past life issues resulting in difficulty bonding with anyone*

☐ *Rejection of life, of God, and of others, as a result of past life experiences*

☐ *Unresolved past life issues between the child and a family member*

☐ *Bonding difficulties, abuse, or neglect experienced by either of the parents in childhood*

☐ *Substance abuse by a parent either during the pregnancy or when the child is young*

☐ *Dislike or lack of interest in children by either parent*

☐ *The parents are from different religious or cultural backgrounds, which can result in some people believing that the relationship is bad. The implication is that there should have been no offspring from the relationship*

☐ *The partners are not fully bonded because one has luggage from a previous relationship or for other reasons*

☐ *A pregnancy at the wrong time, such as soon after the previous one*

☐ *One family member, whether parent, grandparent, or older child in the family,* didn't want the pregnancy, even if only for a few minutes

☐ Pregnancy out of wedlock

☐ The pregnancy is a result of a rape or a sexual relationship with little positive connection

☐ There was physical abuse or neglect in the couple's relationship before, during, or after the birth of the child

☐ Once the soul entered the fetus, the environmental context felt too difficult for the soul

☐ The soul didn't want to incarnate as soon as it did, and felt pressured to do so by its guides. It reacts by withdrawing or being angry

☐ There was insufficient connection between the soul and cells during the pregnancy. This can occur for a variety of reasons

☐ A difficult pregnancy or birth

☐ A child born prematurely and placed in an incubator

☐ Health difficulties during pregnancy or after birth for the mother

☐ Baby is physically ill, has difficulty sleeping, or needs to be hospitalized

☐ *Handicapped child*

☐ *Child is seen as being the "wrong" gender*

☐ *Child is born when the previous child is one and a half to three years old, which results in the previous child feeling dethroned as the "prince" or "princess" in the family*

☐ *Death of a loved one within a year prior to the pregnancy, during the pregnancy, or within the first three years after delivery*

☐ *Post-partum depression*

☐ *The mother returns to work very soon after delivering the baby*

☐ *Colicky baby*

☐ *The father is physically or emotionally unavailable to the mother during the pregnancy and after the child is born*

☐ *Stress or mental health difficulties in one parent*

☐ *Conflict between the parents*

☐ *Financial or other difficulties*

☐ *Adoption or foster care.*

If you think you or your child need healing work to help resolve these issues, the exercises in this book can be done repeatedly for a period of time if you find they continue to help. You can also choose to take the list to a healing practitioner who is able to give you quick results.

There's greater risk of emotional neglect and parent-child conflict, abandonment, or aggression when bonding is weak. We're less likely to tolerate difficulties coming from our child when we're not well-bonded. And as we know, indigos are more of a handful than other children and present us with far more challenges than other children. As a result, a parent may find it difficult to bond with that particular child.

One of the aspects of indigos and other very sensitive souls is that they can feel rejected when there's very little cause to feel that way.

Bonding is a two-way street. Both mother and child need to be well-bonded to each other. It can easily happen that one is strongly bonded and the other much less so.

Bonding can also be damaged at any time in the future for many reasons such as parent-teen conflict, ADHD, mental illness, depression, relationship breakdown, abuse, or substance abuse. Therefore, when you focus on bonding, make sure you heal bonding difficulties throughout your life or your child's, and not only when your child was a baby.

Bonding can be improved over time between a parent and a child through a change in the attitude or behavior of the mother, through healing work, and as a result of difficulties bringing them closer together.

Chapter 3
Bonding and Healing

Interesting research regarding bonding and healing reported by Charlie Fidelman found that premature babies recovered much more quickly from pain induced by medical treatment if they were in very close touch with their mother. Simply being held was insufficient. The greatest benefit to the immune system occurred if the baby was held between the mother's breasts, skin to skin.

Research summarized by Dean Ornish, an eminent researcher on mind-body healing, and many others, has shown that people who are sick recover much more quickly when they're in a positive, loving relationship. They're also less likely to become ill to begin with. People who are single or who are in unhealthy relationships are also more likely to become ill, less likely to recover, or recover more slowly.

Other research summarized by Larry Dossey, who has done excellent work summarizing research on prayer and spirituality, shows that bonding with our Creator and a spiritual group also results in people being healthier and more likely to recover quickly. People who are isolated are more likely to die at a younger age.

Exercise – for you:

Put your right hand on your heart and your left hand on your belly. Imagine warmth coming from above (God, Spirit, sunshine) to your heart, and then to your belly, your inner child. Focus on healing old wounds from when you were small, from when you were rejected at school, or later rejected by a lover. Have Spirit and your heart nurture and heal your inner child.

To make this exercise more powerful and healing, imagine Goddess energy coming in from the universe, through the crown of your head to your heart, to the cellular level, and to your inner child, which is in your belly. Mother Mary, or the very compassionate and healing Kuan Yin from China, work wonderfully well for this. Use one that fits for you, or you can choose to think of the female aspect of God, assuming that God is all things. If you don't believe in God, think of Mother Nature or a woman that you find to be very nurturing and healing from your past.

Exercise – for your child:

If your child suffers from bonding difficulties, hold them to your chest, if they're willing. Fill up your heart center with love and healing energy from above and imagine enveloping your child with it.

If your child is not physically next to you, do it through distance healing by having light go through you, directly to their heart center, and then from Spirit to the crown of their head to their heart center.

Have this profound healing energy go to every level of their being. Focus on areas you know that have been hurt. If your child is old enough or willing, ask them to also do the exercise on themselves.

You can talk about it as you do the healing work if your child is open to it, or after you've finished. If your child is old enough, discuss it with them afterwards. Tell your child you love them and you're sorry for the hurt they've experienced. This doesn't need to imply guilt or blame – it can simply be: "I have sorrow that you've felt bad."

Story:

I had a client, Linda, who complained that her daughter, Patricia, now 27, had been very difficult as a teenager. She acted out a great deal, did drugs, ran away, had boyfriends sneak in through her bedroom window, and her friends broke in and stole from the home a few times. Patricia ended up being sent away to a residential treatment center because nothing else worked.

Patricia gradually improved over time, but was still not doing as well as she could by the time I worked with them.

When I explored the issues, it turned out that Linda almost died right after giving birth and had been kept in the hospital for a few weeks. When I discussed this with them, it turned out that Patricia had known only a bit of this story. She had been deeply impacted by her mother's illness nonetheless. The baby blamed herself for her mother almost dying. This was not at the mental level because her mind wasn't sufficiently developed to think such things at the time. Because this occurred when she was pre-cognitive, before she was five years old, regular forms of therapy were not able to help her heal these issues.

As a result of these difficulties after birth, Patricia withdrew somewhat from her mother. However, Linda also withdrew from Patricia to some degree as well. She had the feeling that her child always wanted too much from her. Her unconscious thought was, "You almost killed me when you were born. You want too much from me."

They showed each other love and caring throughout the daughter's life despite these issues, although the unresolved undercurrents were always there. The result of the unresolved pain for both was that their bonding was not as strong as it otherwise would have been. Because of that, it was very easy

> *for them to get into arguments. Patricia acted out her rage and self-hatred as a teenager, and was sent away from her family to treatment centers as a result. This further added to the bonding difficulties in this family. We were able to heal these issues in a relatively short time.*
>
> *It was wonderful to see both mother and daughter heal and blossom while we worked as a threesome to help resolve the old wounds.*

Men and Bonding

It's common knowledge that a far greater number of men don't bond as deeply in relationships compared with women. Many men are more in touch with anger and much less so with other emotions such as sadness, despair, and joy. This affects their ability to bond with their child and often results in mothers being closer to their children than the fathers. On the other hand, an increasing proportion of men have become sensitive to their emotions and those of others.

Fathers bring a variety of gifts to the family that are as essential as the mother's gifts. For example, research done through Oxford University and reported by Karen Emerton shows that children greatly benefit from fathers reading to them, taking them on outings, playing with them, and taking an interest in their well-being. This doesn't need to be the biological father for the child to benefit, and a divorced father who is involved can also greatly benefit the child.

Research has found that boys with involved fathers are less likely to get in trouble with the police during adolescence. Girls are less likely to have emotional difficulties in adulthood. The children of involved fathers are also likely to do better at school and to have better marriages. Kyle Pruett also found that children with involved fathers are also less likely to become involved with drugs. Fathers also greatly benefit from being more involved with their children.

The role of fathers has become even more important as more and more women have entered the work force over the last few decades, resulting in their having less time for their children. I believe that fathers' involvement is even more important for indigos and other sensitive souls.

In some cases, bonding difficulties occur as a result of the new father being threatened by the pregnancy and the new baby. The baby represents a threat to his connection with his partner. She's now really focused on looking after the baby and recovering from the pregnancy. The husband may then withdraw, become demanding or uncooperative, or act out in other ways. These are clear examples that the father has bonding difficulties of his own from childhood.

Story:

When I worked as a family therapist in child protection, I saw many families in which the teen was acting out and there was parent-teen conflict. As an example of this pattern, I saw a family recently in which the father, John, was very hurt by his daughter Susie's acting out. They had previously been very close. John had unconsciously distanced himself from Susie when she became a budding adolescent, as many fathers do. No more cuddling. At 15, Susie now focused more on friends than on her family, which was normal for her age. Both felt hurt by the reduced connection between them, and both reacted with anger, resulting in their arguing about her friends.

John then reacted by trying to control Susie, making matters worse. Neither of them dealt with the underlying pain of disrupted bonding, which occurred as a result of Susie becoming a young woman. She then acted out her pain, further complicating the situation. The mother, uncertain what to do, reacted by sometimes taking her husband's side when their daughter acted out, and then her daughter's side when he was too firm. This complicated matters as well. All that was needed to heal the hurt was to help them see what was going on and to help them heal the hurt that resulted from Susie growing up. The parents could then adjust to Susie's growth and need for independence more appropriately. In some cases, it takes very little effort to help resolve these types of difficulties, although they're far more complex in other cases.

Bonding and Older Children

For an overview of adolescence in general, I refer you to a university textbook called "Adolescence" by John Santrock.

In summarizing the research on bonding and adolescence, Laura Canetti, in a professional journal called "Adolescence," discussed research by her and her colleagues that found that many adolescent mental health concerns are attributed to difficulties in bonding between parent and child. Research has shown that lack of a supportive and accepting environment correlates with poor mental and behavioral adjustment.

In addition, research has shown that the greater the youth's orientation toward peers and away from parents, the more they're likely to be depressed.

As Gordon Neufeld and Gabor Maté have stated in "Hold On To Your Kids" (page 6), "For a child well attached to us, we are her home base from which to venture into the world, her retreat to fall back to. All the parenting skills in the world cannot compensate for a lack of attachment relationship. All the love in the world cannot get through without the psychological umbilical cord created by the child's attachment."

Story:

I've worked with many families in which the mother must work long hours to make ends meet.

As an example, I worked with a single mother and her 16-year-old son, Joe. The family had previously had financial difficulties and the mother, Amanda, had to return to work soon after birth and worked 12 hours a day. Their financial situation improved a few years later. However, when he became a teen, Joe still had the unresolved pain of his going to daycare beginning a month after birth, as well as his mother being unavailable much of the time because of her long work hours. He still carried that pain as well as his mother's guilt at having sent him to daycare so young.

As a result of her guilt, Amanda let Joe get away with more than she otherwise would have. The result is that he kept pushing her for more as a way of trying to feel fulfillment from her, to fill the hole from his infancy. Both became frustrated with each other, and the conflict would escalate to the point where they would yell at each other and Joe became uncooperative. Amanda would then feel guilty and let Joe have whatever he wanted. This became part of the problem.

When I worked with them, it was a simple matter to help the family see that Joe had unresolved bonding issues and Amanda had unresolved guilt as a result of feeling she had abandoned her baby soon after birth to go to work, as well as long work hours over the years. I assisted them to heal these and helped the mother to set healthy boundaries. The problems were then quickly resolved.

As I mentioned earlier, I believe that because they're
so sensitive, indigos are more easily affected by bonding
issues than other people are. This is partly why many
indigos become more independent from their parents during
adolescence and become more closely bonded with their
peers, who don't have the ability to guide them wisely.

Broader Issues

Consider your situation. Do you have positive
relationships with your spouse or partner and your child
much of the time? How about with your extended family?
With friends? Do you expect that life will feed and support
you or do you spend much of your time worrying about
paying the bills? Do you give up on projects very easily
when difficulties occur?

Bonding difficulties can have a broad impact on us
beyond our close relationships. They may also impact your
child at school. Your child may have unresolved emotional
pain and so have difficulty concentrating, may think of
learning as being irrelevant because they feel empty inside,
or may be more interested in connecting with peers than in
taking their responsibilities. They may also become bullied
because they're seen as an easy target, as a result of feeling
and acting small. As with other issues, these concerns tend
to be amplified with indigos because they're so sensitive and
strong-willed.

Parenting Issues

One of the aspects that we need to consider is that the
vast majority of indigos are more advanced as souls than

their parents. Some parents react by being jealous of their children. Others react by trying to suppress them. Still others react by giving in too much because their child is so powerful, or catering to them too much because of their child's sensitivity.

My perspective is that many indigos are part of a very extended soul group, many of whom are warrior souls. As many have said, indigos have come to help change the world.

One of the aspects is that the parents may also be part of the same or different soul type – such as also being warrior souls but at a less advanced level. They might also be different types of souls. For example, my orientation is that of a healer and very emotional whereas my son's style is more cognitive and scientific. This has posed challenges in our bonding and connection.

These issues can easily result in conflict between indigos and their parents. This can also occur between indigos and other authority figures. For example, they may have their way of doing things and don't want to change to accommodate a child's needs and perspective.

As I mentioned earlier, indigos don't respond well to parents or other authority figures that are either quite laid back or controlling. What's needed is authoritative parenting, a combination of caring and firmness. They need our guidance but without having it forced on them. They also need their parents and other authority figures to express themselves clearly with them. For example, they want to understand why we say no to their request, rather than just being told no – and it needs to make sense to them.

Being involved with indigos forces many of us as their parents, teachers, and helpers to grow and become more open and honest, to know our mind and express it, and to have clear boundaries and be prepared to say no. In other words, although indigos are not part of our soul groups, they're here to help us and other adults to grow beyond our comfort zone. It just makes things worse for them and for us if we refuse to hear them and resist their attempts to make this a better home, a better school, and a better world.

On the other hand, indigos also need to learn and grow from us, and it's not appropriate to give in to whatever they want. I was recently involved with an indigo who thought it was her job to tell me what to do and push me around so that I'd be a better person from her perspective. Her attempts to control me did not go over well with me. It's not appropriate for us to force our wisdom on someone else. Free will is crucial. Although our children may think their perspective is right and we're completely wrong, they don't always know what the wisest thing is to do either for themselves or for us, as the next story illustrates.

Story:

Over the years, I've seen all kinds of family dramas that gradually escalated more and more over time. The following is a case I worked with to do a custody assessment for the courts. The child in this case, Lisa, nine years old at the time, was certainly not always an innocent victim. She had unresolved insecure bonding issues because her parents had been arguing with each other for a number of years, before and after their marital separation. The parents had unresolved bonding issues from their childhoods as well. They put less energy than was needed in the care of their child before the separation and for about a year afterwards, while they were grieving and arguing with each other.

Although I didn't discuss this with them directly, I could tell intuitively that they knew each other very well at the soul level, and had spent many lifetimes together. However, the pattern at the soul group level was that soul group members experienced a great deal of conflict with each other lifetime after lifetime. Lisa felt bad for her parents because of all their pain, and she tried to do a variety of things to help them feel better. However, her assistance was done in such a way that it made things much worse.

Lisa, an indigo, would tell her father how bad mom was as a way of showing him support and that she was on his side. Then, at mom's home, she would tell her mom how bad dad was as a way of showing mom that she was very close to her. Both parents were happy to hear these positives about their connection with their child and the negatives about the other parent, thus reinforcing their child's behavior.

Both ended up feeling that their poor daughter was being terribly victimized in the other home. This escalated their fight and the matter went to court, *where they both wanted to gain sole custody and limited access for the other parent. Both ended up calling child protection services against each other several times, as well as bringing in other professionals to take their side.*

Because Lisa had allergies and stress due to the bind she and her parents were in, each parent took Lisa to a separate physician, and each parent indirectly asked their physician to take their side and make recommendations that would fit their view against the other parent. The physicians weren't aware of each other's involvement or how their information was used to fuel the conflict between the parents, to the detriment of the family and of the child.

Over time, more and more professionals became involved, and the courts had no way of determining what was actually going on in these two homes. I was asked to provide a custody assessment in this case. I was able to determine that both homes were adequately healthy for the child's well-being, but the problem was the child's acting out, and the parents' willingness to believe that the other parent was bad without checking out what the child said. This resulted in the situation going out of control. It was the connection between the two homes through the child, helping professionals, and the courts which was the problem. The bottom line was that the child had enormous power in this family

> *because her parents simply believed what she said*
> *about the other home without checking it out.*

It is possible to assist in healing these various issues if approached the right way and if the parties are willing to do the healing work. Yet many separated couples are unwilling to do this and prefer to see the worst in each other. The result is that they can fight for years, to each other's detriment as well as to the child's, who is caught in the middle between the parents. As research discussed by Constance Ahrons in "The Good Divorce" has shown, 25% of separated spouses with children fight with each other for years.

Chapter 4
Bonding and Our Soul

Research has shown that the quality of our relationship with our parents impacts how we view our relationship with God. For example, a child who has angry parents will perceive God as being angry and vengeful.

We can heal unresolved bonding issues toward our parents, our spouse, and toward God by connecting with Spirit. As I mentioned before, define Spirit as you will. The result, as we grow more and more fully, is that we can give unconditionally to a greater and greater extent and, in the process, need less from others. And then we don't need to get caught up in our partner's or child's difficulties, and we can assist them more when they're in pain or give them the space they need to heal their own issues.

The following is a wonderful way of healing bonding difficulties. I recommend you try this exercise even if you were very well nurtured as a child. Even healing slight wounds from childhood can help us to become a more whole human being.

Exercise:

Imagine Goddess energy coming in from above through the top of your head and into every cell in your body. This is effortless. All you have to do is to have the intention and to be aware. Spirit does the rest. Have Goddess energy heal the sense of abandonment, deprivation, and fear that you carry. Have the energy go into your belly, your inner child.

I find Mother Mary to be very healing and nurturing if you're comfortable using her energy. You can also choose to use Kuan Yin from China or Lakshmi from India. Or you can experiment with your own favorite. If you don't believe in God, you can think of a very nurturing woman you've known or you can connect with nurturing from Mother Earth. Imagine that this energy is helping you to heal, and imagine that this energy becomes part of who you are. For example, you become more nurturing yourself, like Goddess energy, although you also have God energy. Remember, we're part of all that is and so we have both a fragment of God and Goddess energy within us.

Try this exercise for five or ten minutes. See how you feel now as compared to before the exercise. If it feels really nurturing and healing, consider doing this

---

> *every day for the next month or so to help you heal*
> *more and more deeply over time. Heal resistances*
> *to bonding as they arise.*
>
> *Many of us who've had difficult childhoods*
> *will avoid this exercise like the plague – because*
> *we feel we don't deserve it, and for many other*
> *reasons. Be aware of that – and decide who's the*
> *boss – you or those dark under-layers we all carry.*
> *And act accordingly. Just be aware that some of*
> *these immature under-layers that we carry are very*
> *persistent and are quite difficult to heal. When this*
> *occurs to you, make use of the exercises I mentioned*
> *in the last section regarding reverse polarity.*

Bonding and Our Soul Journey

The discussion thus far has focused on bonding as it relates to the neurological, psychological, and relationship levels. These are essential. However, to get a thorough picture regarding bonding, we must also take into consideration issues that relate to the soul and soul group levels.

Some people, including myself, believe that we have some choice regarding where and when we're born, although our guides help us with this. We set a contract at the soul level with our future parents before the pregnancy. This is true even if they'll give us up at birth or abuse or neglect us later. We agreed to go through these experiences for our growth as a soul. Of course, most of us aren't in touch with our soul very much and we don't remember these soul agreements.

The result of this is that although we want to be in this particular family at the soul level, our personality may absolutely hate it. We're torn, often without even realizing that we are. Of course, all of this is relative – we may have mixed feelings at the soul level, as well as at the personality level. My view is that if we had none of these issues, we wouldn't need to incarnate again to work them through. We'd simply be part of the Godhead.

The reality is that all of us come down to earth with unresolved issues from previous lifetimes. These unresolved issues are stored in our causal body, which is connected to our soul. It's the part of us that carries our luggage, our positive and negative karma, from one lifetime to the next. Our soul is pure but needs to learn lessons and evolve over the course of lifetimes.

One of the aspects of choosing where we're born is our soul age. Some writers suggest that younger souls don't have the wisdom to choose where to be born and so it's selected for them by their guides. Old souls and indigos decide where and when to be born with the help of their guides, or guardian angels as some people call them.

As I discussed earlier, souls sometimes make a mistake about where to be born. In some cases, the situation feels much worse than they had realized before coming into the incarnation. As a result, some souls don't want to bond with their parents and with the world. They reject it. If that happens with your child, the result is that they will not want to be with you, will not want to do chores or homework, and may not want to do much that's constructive in life. They may be angry at being here and act that out. Or a teen or adult may get into prescription drugs for anxiety or depression, or alcohol or illegal drugs, in order to escape.

Although bonding difficulties are not the only cause of becoming alcoholic or taking drugs, in my experience bonding and loss are two of the most important issues, along with unresolved issues toward God.

Some of these unresolved issues toward God may include the following, among others: anger toward God at the soul level for past grievances, withdrawing as a result of feeling unworthy of serving, or shutting down in relation to other people as a result of not trusting that we're safe in the world because we felt at the soul level that God wasn't there for us in the past. These unresolved issues all greatly affect the family interactions. These issues can result in what is called a "dark night of the soul," when we're depressed or in angst, and can't find a solution. What needs to be done here is to surrender all expectations of God, to go into the great mystery and abandon all need to control our lives, and accept all that comes to us. This results in surrendering our ego more and more.

Sometimes, we're born before we've done the healing we needed to do from the previous lifetime. The soul may have been overly eager to come back in an incarnation to do some work. More often, souls are gently pushed by their guides to be incarnated again before they feel fully ready.

With souls who are particularly close to each other, what some people call soul mates, everything is intensified. For example, we so yearn for union with that soul that a small rejection is experienced as being devastating. This all gets acted out in the dyad and in the family as a whole.

Since indigos are more in touch with their souls than are young, mature, and old souls, all those issues are closer to the surface and are amplified for them. I've seen many indigos who struggled with anxiety and other feelings that resulted from past life issues being close to the surface.

Story:

In most families, each soul has unresolved karma with the other souls. Think of George and Helen, a couple. They felt very connected as people and as souls in the first few years. Their connection from previous lifetimes made them feel like they knew each other very deeply and they felt great together from day one.

After a while, they started having a bit of conflict now and then. Their distrust for each other gradually increased. This activated unresolved issues from their previous lifetimes together, which added fuel to the fire without their realizing it.

And then a child was born to this couple. For many couples, having a child brings them closer together and results in the burying of their difficulties for a time, perhaps even until the child leaves home. In this case, they have a child, Samantha, an indigo, who takes a great deal of space in her family.

Samantha is highly sensitive and intensely feels the negativity between her parents. Partly as a result of this, she has many temper tantrums when she's small. This increases the difficulties between George and Helen, and they begin to have power struggles in terms of how to handle their child. Samantha, feeling her parents' conflict intensely, cries loudly whenever there's conflict between them. This further increases the stress in the family.

As a soul, Samantha is more connected with her father than with her mother because they've spent more lifetimes together, and he lets her get away with more than mom does. As a result, as she grows up, Samantha takes the side of her father against her mother when there's conflict between them. Helen reacts by telling her, "You're just like your dad."

When Samantha is 12, her parents separate and she ends up living with her mother. She's angry that she was abandoned by her dad. She's also angry because she has to stay with her mom. She doesn't like this because she's not highly bonded with her mother. On top of that, her mom doesn't let her get away with as much as her dad does.

Helen is still angry with Samantha for having taken her father's side whenever there were disagreements between the couple. On top of that, she was able to manipulate dad to get more freedom than mom thought was appropriate. The result is that the conflict between mother and daughter increases after the separation, and Samantha begins to act out more and more as their conflict escalates. This further activates the unresolved conflict between them from previous lifetimes, which adds fuel to the fire.

Samantha complains to dad about how badly mom treats her. She tells him that mom grabbed her and shook her, although she doesn't say that she did the same to her mom – that they were having a shoving and shouting match. As a result, dad contacts child protection services to check out the mother's home. This deepens the conflict between the couple and the mother feels victimized by Samantha, who wants to go live with her dad even more than before.

However, this isn't possible because he's got a new girlfriend who's not interested in having Samantha in their lives. Dad's girlfriend is also jealous when he spends time with Samantha. He spends less time with Samantha to placate his girlfriend, but feels guilty about it. The result of Samantha seeing her dad very little is that she feels abandoned by him. She then blames her mother for having, in her view, caused the family break-up, and her losing her father in the process.

The conflict escalates further between mother and daughter, and Samantha runs away on occasion. George calls child protection regularly, in part because he feels guilty that he's not as involved in Samantha's life as he knows he needs to be. Samantha eventually ends up in a foster home, and remains there for a few years. Helen is seen by George, Samantha, and the authorities as being an unfit parent. She questions herself as well, but the fact is that she is a competent parent and there's a triangle between the family members which is replaying itself in this lifetime.

This is an example where the child protection authorities get caught up in the family's dysfunctional patterns and take over the parenting role, rather than assist in the healing work. I've seen this happen over and over with parent-teen conflict and acting out teens when I worked as a family therapist in a child protection setting.

In this scenario, this is a repetition from previous lifetimes of the closeness between father and daughter, in which they exclude the mother. It's also a repetition of old conflict between mother and father from previous lifetimes. It also plays out old rejections and conflict that Samantha and her mother experienced in previous lifetimes. Rather than resolving the issues, they replay them and add to their negative karma through their unhealthy interactions in this lifetime.

What would be very useful to help resolve the difficulties in this particular case are the following:

- *Assist in healing the unresolved issues in all three parties, beginning at the soul and soul group level, if they're open to this. If not, do it while working with one of the clients, and include a focus on distance healing for the others. Go to the next exercise on pages 332 to 334 for a reminder on how to do distance healing.*

- *Three aspects need to be dealt with – the soul level, between souls, and within the soul group. Get them to do a visualization of unresolved issues at the seat of the soul from previous lifetimes, as well as at the causal body. Ask Spirit to transform this old karma for each individual as well as between souls.*

- *Help the daughter transform the negative energy she's carrying from her parents' conflict, beginning when she was in the uterus. This needs to be done at the cellular level and in the various layers of her aura.*

- *Help resolve the conflict between the parents, if both are willing, and help get the daughter out of the triangle she's caught in between them.*

- *Improve the bonding between mother and daughter, as part of helping to resolve the anger and distrust between them.*

- *Assist the father to see that he's part of the problem when he complains about the mother being inappropriate and encourages his daughter to rebel against her mother. He's also part of the problem by refusing to provide a home for his daughter except for an occasional weekend visit.*

- *Help father and daughter to spend more time together.*

- *Help the parents determine how these patterns fit their experience in their families of origin, and assist in healing those.*

- *Help the daughter to see that she's playing into the conflict between her parents and sacrificing her life in the process.*

- *Help the father's girlfriend to see that her partner would be more emotionally available to her if he didn't feel pressured to stay away from his daughter.*

- *Help the child protection worker to see that the family is much healthier than the worker had previously realized, and assist the parents in reintegrating their daughter back into either home, or split her care between them.*

As you can see, for any or all family members to visit an individual therapist, most of the issues between the individuals would remain unresolved. Working on the mother's anger, or the father's guilt, or the daughter's feeling abandoned, would not change any of the family problems.

Family therapy is ideal for helping to resolve these types of difficulties. However, although family therapy is very useful at helping to shift relationships, it is quite unhelpful to heal either emotional trauma or issues at the soul level. Other approaches are needed for those aspects. It's possible for the family to work with different professionals to assist in resolving each of these issues, although it's far more effective for the family to work with one professional who can assist with all of it if such a professional were available to the family.

Although I listed quite a few options above, many others could be used, depending on who's willing or not willing to do the work, the individuals' soul ages, and on other factors. Although this may sound very complicated to you, this type of work often requires no more than six to eight sessions of 90 to 120 minutes each, and sometimes twelve. It generally takes longer if there's also been abuse or neglect in the family.

In the research we did on the effectiveness of my work as a family therapist with child protection clients, our rate of effectiveness was 86%, as high as any other program in North America, and with an average of less than nine sessions averaging one and a half hours each (Thivierge, 1988, 1995). Our work did not take into account healing at the soul level at that time, and so research on our work with these clients would almost certainly take somewhat longer and would prove to be more effective.

Family therapy and healing work, including at the soul level if people are open to it, is very cost effective rather than "storing" children and youth in foster care or other care facilities for years. The result of that approach from child protection creates further trauma and further dysfunction when the "warehoused children" grow up into being parents themselves. Needless to say, some children need to be placed in foster homes, group homes, or treatment centers. However, my experience is that most do not because the problems can most often be resolved quite quickly, and at a far lower cost.

This is just one example out of a multitude of possible scenarios in which soul-related issues impact a family. However, this gives you a feel for the process. Soul connection between family members can either increase positive or negative energy, or both, in a variety of ways.

In my follow-up book on indigos and their families, I'll give you many examples of various types of family difficulties and this will help you to assess your own family situation. Please remember that most people tend to be very aware of others' roles in family difficulties while being blind to their own.

Exercise:

Here's how you can heal some of the issues at the soul and soul group level, as in the previous example. I'll write this exercise for immediate family members. However, you can use this for relationship difficulties with anyone.

Focus on the bonding issue: Have light go in from above through the top of your head to your heart center. Have it go down to your belly and heal your inner child.

Focus on your own healing to begin with: Apart from unresolved trauma and other issues mentioned in the previous section, let's assume you have unresolved negativity between the two of you from previous lifetimes, an assumption that's probably accurate in most cases. You can do this whether it's fear, anger, distrust, or other negative emotions or perceptions. Focus on six inches (15 centimeters) over the top of your head, which is called the seat of the soul, or higher self. Ask Spirit to remove negativity that you carry there from previous lifetimes regarding a particular relationship difficulty. Ask that it also be removed from your causal body. Also check to see if this was a pattern in your family of origin. If so, ask Spirit to resolve it for your family members as well. Do distance healing for them, as described below.

Focus on distance healing of the other person, whether it is your child, spouse, parent, or someone else. Resolve your negative feelings toward the other person first, using the exercises in the previous section, such as Ho'oponopono, the butterfly hug, or a visualization. You then do distance healing by forming a triangle with Spirit. Imagine light coming in through the top of your head to your heart center, which is at the center of your chest. Fill up your heart center. Imagine light going from your heart to the other person's heart center. Now, ask for light to come in from above to the top of the other person's

---

head and into their heart center. You then ask that their issues be healed regarding this particular relationship concern. For example, ask that the other person's anger or distrust be resolved from previous lifetimes. Ask that it be resolved at the seat of the soul, soul group level, cellular level, family of origin, and DNA if it's a broad pattern. You can do this directly with the other person if they're open to it.

Healing energy between people: Continuing with this exercise, ask Spirit to clear the space between the seat of your soul, six inches (15 centimeters) over your head, and the seat of the other person's soul. Ask that negativity be transformed at all levels between you, and particularly between your heart centers.

Now check and see how you feel as compared to before the exercise.

Soul Group Patterns

Our soul group members are all at approximately the same level of development, just as students in grade seven are at very similar levels. As I discussed in the first section, indigos are at a higher level of soul development than are old souls. Most of their parents are old souls, and a small minority are indigos.

In addition, as I mentioned in the first section, some old soul women choose young soul men to be with to look after them because they're unwilling or feel unable to manage their own lives. As a result, some fathers and stepfathers of indigos are younger souls. In my experience, those men tend to try to be very controlling toward their indigos, and this generally works poorly and sometimes has very damaging results. Some women also try to be controlling toward their indigos, and this generally works poorly as well. Doing healing work at the soul level does not work for either young souls or mature souls because they don't have the understanding, interest, or capacity to do so. However, some people have the capacity but are not interested in doing healing work at the soul level.

Before we incarnate, we have an agreement as to what our relationship will be like. For example, we've made the agreement to give each other limited caring and to reject each other, thus providing each of us with opportunities to work through this issue. Thus, we not only attract and manifest rejection in this lifetime because that's how, unconsciously, we believe we should be treated, but we plan for it before we're born.

This is true with other types of family themes as well, such as control and dominance, giving a great deal without looking after our own needs, irresponsibility by one spouse and over-functioning by the other, financial difficulties, illness, and so on. Some broader themes play themselves out over and over in a variety of our relationships until we learn what needs to be learned. It becomes harder and harder to keep blaming others for our relationship problems over and over again with different people. However, mature souls and younger ones keep doing that and avoid taking responsibility for their lives. Once we heal the underlying causes and decide we don't want that in our lives any more, we can begin functioning at a higher level.

All of us need to learn to be more in our power and take full responsibility for our lives. We also need to open our heart more and more. As part of this, we need to learn to fully accept ourselves and our various family members, and to give them love in the process. Otherwise, we'll replay some of the same dances next lifetime.

In my practice, many of the people I work with are bodhisattvas in training. Many of you readers are at that level of development as well. As you'll remember from the first section, these are advanced souls who focus on helping to resolve the suffering of others as much as possible. What happens with many of them is that they forget about self-care in the process of looking after others and then they end up running out of gas.

Others become outraged that there's so much suffering and become angry with God. Others are frustrated or feel like failures because other people simply won't listen to their advice on how to lead better lives.

A large majority of the bodhisattva souls I've worked with absorb a great deal of other people's suffering and their light gets dimmed in the process. They do so because they don't know how or don't take the time to protect themselves energetically and get in their power, as we discussed earlier on page 137.

These are typical patterns with many bodhisattva level souls that I've seen and many of their soul groups. Many old souls and indigos will not be able to relate to these issues because they haven't arrived at that level of development yet.

One of the things I do with these bodhisattvas is to assist to resolve the issues not only with my clients, but also within and between each soul group member, as well as for their ancestors. I also assist many old souls and indigos to resolve the patterns at their soul group level as well.

When we grow a great deal in one lifetime, we can end up outgrowing our soul group. One option is for us to leave our soul group and go to a higher level of functioning. That's valid. However, I believe the wiser goal is to help them grow as well so that they'll come up with us if they wish to. We can't control them or take responsibility for them. However, it's important that we take appropriate steps to help them grow if they wish to.

So you see, we tend to have the same issues to work through at all levels, down here at the human level as well as at the soul level, As I mentioned earlier, Hermes' law of the universe states, "as above so below, as within so without." Our duty here is to help each other learn our lessons, if they wish to do so. All of us have blind spots and need help to progress. Family relationships are an opportunity to heal all these issues. So are soul group relationships. So are extended soul groups, which are like extended family.

In summary, with a broad theme in our lives, such as rejection and abandonment, we're affected at all levels:

- at the relationship level – family of origin, friends, spouse, and perhaps with our children as well;

- with our inner child – as we feel rejected or abused by others, for example, we tend to treat ourselves harshly, judging ourselves, rejecting our needs, and so on;

- at the cellular level and in our DNA, which relates to historical trauma from our ancestors;

- at the soul level, including old karma and past lives; and

- at the soul group and extended soul group levels.

It's important for us to understand at which of these levels we have unresolved issues, and resolve them at the appropriate levels.

If your child has a difficulty with a school for example, it's useful for you to consider whether this is part of a broader pattern or not. If your child is bullied at school, it's important to look at it from a number of angles. Does your child have difficulties with being pushed around in other areas of their lives as well? Have you or your spouse been bullied in the past or been treated badly by others on a regular basis over the course of your life? Were you born in a cultural group that's been pushed around a great deal over centuries? If it's a broad pattern, you can be sure that it's also an issue at the soul level as well as at the soul group level.

The bottom line is that when negativity happens to us, it's important to think of it as either that we're working through old karma or that it's a lesson we need to learn. Thinking like a victim wastes our time and simply creates more pain. Let's learn to take responsibility for our lives more fully and teach it to our kids as well. In the process, we can all help to make the world a better place.

Chapter 5
A Bodhisattva Journey

My strong conviction is that all of us, but especially old souls, indigos, and other sensitive souls, can do a great deal to help heal the world. Parents of indigo children can greatly help them to do their share. If we or our children ignore the calling of our soul to heal more and more and to help others, we pay by suffering from mental, emotional, physical and relationship difficulties.

If you're the parent of a small child, you can ask their soul to help to heal the world. You can test this out by asking their soul to send you healing energy. Once you can feel that this works, you can then ask your baby or small child to send healing energy anywhere – to a sick family member, to a country in difficulty, etc. Older children can participate directly with your assistance.

As we become more and more advanced as souls, it's our responsibility to help heal other people, the world, and the various creatures and plants in it. As we advance further and further, we can broaden our perspective more and more regarding the nature of healing to the point where it becomes very multi-dimensional. For a variety of ideas and methods on multi-dimensional healing, go to page 138 and to the section entitled The Really Tough Stuff beginning on page 261.

Here's a brief example of multi-dimensional healing that I experienced. I went on a healing journey to Haiti in the summer of 2010. As almost everyone knows, about a quarter of a million people lost their lives there because of the earthquake in January of that year, and 1.5 million people lost their homes. If you want more information about this project, and how you could choose to help, go to www.phoenixvision.org.

The way I became involved started a couple of days after the earthquake. While I was meditating I got the inspiration that I should go to Haiti.

I got confirmation of that message from Spirit twenty minutes later. Three young women were in the park at the seawall near my home with a video camera. One of them asked me if I would mind being interviewed, but without telling me what the focus was. I hesitated, but said OK. They got the tape rolling and asked me: "What do you plan to do about Haiti?" I took this as confirmation from Spirit that I should go. A few days later, a woman approached me and asked me to give money for the children in Haiti because they didn't have water. I told her I don't give money on the street (although I do buy meals and other things for street people fairly regularly). She said it wasn't for her but to send the money directly. I took this as further confirmation that I should go.

I decided to go six months after the earthquake, after most of the dust had settled because most people who are traumatized get back on their feet within three or four months after a disaster. I wanted to help those who continued to be really stuck. As you know by now, my career focuses especially on helping people who continue to be stuck despite trying many things to resolve their difficulties.

I discussed this with a number of people and six people decided to come with me. We discussed what needed to be done and practiced the healing methods I discuss in this book, among others. We sent healing energy to the people, the land, those who had passed over, and so on. As a result, we became attacked energetically from Haiti and other sources. All of us were negatively impacted. I was able to resolve some of this but I hadn't learned how to resolve some forms of attacks yet. Over time, all six trainees withdrew for various reasons but the bottom line was that the attacks were too hard on them. It's not surprising that they withdrew given that, not only were they attacked, but so was their connection with me. Unfortunately, I hadn't learned how to master those issues yet.

As a result of dealing with these difficulties, I developed more and more expertise on how to resolve them as a result of scanning and asking Spirit for guidance and help. I learned that I was being attacked by voodoo curses, which is practiced in Haiti, as well as energy from the dark side of Atlantis, which had existed near Haiti until about 2500 years ago near Haiti. I also picked up entities from people who passed over during the earthquake as well as death energy from the people who died.

I was also impacted by historical trauma from the people and the land, including the following issues, among others. For example, when Christopher Columbus first arrived to the Americas, his ship foundered and he was rescued by the locals. He soon turned them all into slaves to mine for gold. Because they were grossly overworked and as a result of illnesses that the Europeans had brought with them, such as chicken pox, all the indigenous people died within a few decades.

The Spanish then replaced this labor force by bringing in slaves from Africa. Many died in the ships coming over because of the terrible conditions. Most of the survivors died from overwork before being able to reproduce because it was cheaper to bring in new slaves than to raise the children of slaves until they could be productive. The French eventually took over the island but were just as harsh as the Spanish. The slaves eventually rebelled successfully against the French. Other countries, such as Britain, tried to invade Haiti, but with no success.

Haiti is the only country in written history to have successfully fought for its freedom from slavery. However, the international community didn't want their slaves to learn about Haiti's successful fight against oppression. As a result, Haiti was completely shut out by the international community. All of this devastated Haiti's economy and it became and still is to this day the poorest country in the Americas.

One of the factors is that Haiti is struck by hurricanes and other natural disasters far more than other countries that are close by, even fifty miles away – such as Cuba. Environmental factors such as mountains don't account for this. This suggests to me that there are other negative energies that are causing the difficulties in Haiti. I've taken some steps to begin to resolve those, although far more energy work is needed by many people to help resolve this, as well as the country's other difficulties.

As I connected more and more with Haiti energetically before going, I came to be affected by all the despair, hatred, prejudice, and other negativity that is still in Haiti.

With experimentation and guidance, I learned how to heal all those issues. For example, I had experienced a ritualized curse in the past, but never from voodoo. I realized after a while that I needed to send positive voodoo energy to counteract the negative voodoo energy.

I was still determined to go and do my best to help uplift the people, in part by helping to free them from these negative energies. What I learned from dealing with these various energies before going to Haiti turned out to be invaluable because they prepared me to deal with these issues successfully when I got there.

Among other things, I did the following before I went and while I was there:

- Sent healing energy in general while also healing myself;

- Sent healing energy to my DNA, to my soul, and to my soul group in terms of issues relating to oppression, enslavement, and enslaving others in past lives;

- Sent energy to those who died, and those who survived but were suffering from trauma and other issues;

- Sent energy to their DNA to help to heal historical trauma – slavery, previous destructive politics, hurricanes, etc.;

- Sent healing energy to the people who'd withdrawn from our project;

- Sent healing energy to the land. I learned to address some of the negative issues specifically, for example, I sent healing energy regarding the historical trauma that I mentioned earlier;

- Sent healing energy to higher beings who are connected with this land who have been wounded in Haiti in previous lifetimes or at other times;

- Asked high beings, such as Krishna, Christ, Buddha, Archangels, Kuan Yin, Mother Mary, other Goddesses, positive extra-terrestrials, bodhisattvas, and saints, among others, for help with this healing work.

I sent positive energy from positive souls from Atlantis, which had previously been near Haiti, to counteract negative energy from dark Atlanteans that had become connected with Haiti in the past.

I sent energy from Christ and Mother Mary because the area is mostly Catholic, with some Protestants. Since most people are also connected with the positive side of the voodoo religion to some degree, I also made use of energy from the positive side of voodoo.

When I arrived in Haiti, I still had no idea what I was to do although my goal was to be as helpful as possible in helping to heal the situation. I had tried to connect with various people and organizations and made no headway except for a bed and breakfast to go to when I arrived. I went in walking into the unknown. My belief is that I had been blocked from either positive or negative energies or both from being connected before I went. I was determined to go no matter what because of the guidance I had received. I surrendered the path, the method, and the focus to Spirit. I asked to be guided step by step.

I hired a driver who was connected to the bed and breakfast I stayed at to give me a tour of the area hit by the earthquake, the day after I arrived in Haiti. This included visiting a number of tent cities where people lived because they had lost their homes. I sent healing energy around me as we went. And I asked the high beings to assist with the healing as well. Remember what Jesus said – ask and you shall receive. To only send my own healing energy in such a devastated area would have had little impact. It was crucial to work with a great many high beings if I was to have any impact at all.

My driver, Aventu, and I first went up the mountain next to Port-au-Prince to get an overview of the earthquake zone. I was inspired to buy a little sculpture of the 'Marron Inconnu,' a small copy of the original which is in the center of downtown, across from the destroyed parliament buildings. This is a sculpture of an escaped slave who still has a shackle and chain around his ankle. He also has a sword in his hand and is calling out to the masses to stand up for freedom. I felt this was a fabulous symbol for Haiti, which fought for and gained its freedom from European oppression in 1804. This is also a wonderful symbol for other oppressed and downtrodden people around the world – and for us all.

When I got downtown, I saw thousands of tents and little shacks in which people lived. People there are provided with only water and toilets. They're given no food or other services because the United Nations has labeled this as an unsafe zone. Aventu showed me the tip of the Marron Inconnu, which was totally surrounded by tents. He asked me if I'd like to take a photo of it. Yes. As I was taking a picture, a woman asked me if I'd like to see her home, a little shack. I got a tour of her pitiful home, met her children, and left.

Ten minutes later, I realized that I'd been guided there and went back. I told this woman that I'd come to Haiti to provide trauma healing and wasn't sure what I would be doing yet. If she'd like, I told her I'd be happy to work with a group if she'd like to bring one together. Yes. I said no more than a dozen adults and half a dozen children. She agreed and, once they came together, I did healing work with them – including asking them what they'd gone through, and showing them healing visualizations and the butterfly hug, along with making use of their own spiritual practices – prayer and singing songs to God. I told them that they should connect with Spirit in a way that fits for them. I was not here to sell them particular beliefs or methods. I also reminded them that we're all brothers and sisters no matter what our beliefs – that we need to pray for and support each other.

This group session worked out very well. At the end of this first meeting, a woman from the group said she could bring together a second group. I asked her to please do so. I ended up with four groups like this within a few days. Spirit was clearly guiding me because I was wanting to serve with no agenda – open and surrendering to the needs of the people and higher guidance.

Our work unfolded from there and I ended up assisting about 50 women and their children. In addition to the healing work I did with the people, I also did community development to assist them to become organized and work together. I also provided them with micro-financing to assist them to get on their feet. When they pay the money back, it then gets loaned to another person. It costs only $65 to assist one of these women and their children to develop a small business and become self-sufficient.

In summary, the goals of this project are to help to heal people's trauma, to help resolve negative energies that oppress them, to do community development to assist them to help each other, and to provide micro-financing to help them start small businesses so they can be self-sufficient. If sufficient money comes in, we hope to buy land for them so they can move, and help them to build houses and other infrastructure.

After I went back home, a number of people became involved with the Haiti project. Some are planning to go with me on my next trip in December 2010 or on later trips. They have full knowledge as to the difficulties that I and previous trainees experienced and I'm training them on how to resolve those more fully.

It's an option for other people to help out with this project, no matter where they live in the world. People can help in a great many ways, as can be seen on my article on the subject at http://phoenixvision.org/HaitiArticle%20810.pdf. People can choose to donate, do work from home, or go to Haiti with our group. Please feel free to contact us if you're interested in this project.

We'll later expand this project to other countries.

I'm giving you a thumbnail sketch of our work in Haiti as an example of what all of us as bodhisattvas and old souls can do, and what might be involved in trying to help resolve difficulties in some of the darkest corners of the world. I'm not proposing you go into the darkest places. In fact, I recommend that it may be best for you to gain mastery helping people who suffer near where you live before you tackle such difficult places as Haiti unless you're trained and closely supervised.

Although I certainly wasn't expecting anything for me from my work in Haiti, I've gained tremendous benefits spiritually. And my healing work with clients has greatly deepened and speeded up. I'm very grateful to Spirit for having guided me to go there.

Conclusion

You can choose to believe or not believe the comments, recommendations, and stories in this book. It's entirely up to you. However, if you keep trying behavior management, medication, and other traditional Western methods in an attempt to improve your life or that of your indigo child but aren't making progress, I recommend that you consider broadening your perspective. Challenges are introduced into our lives as an opportunity to grow and to heal more and more fully. Avoiding taking the needed steps only intensifies our struggle against the universe's guidance.

As an example of a failed attempt to help in this area, I worked with a fundamentalist Christian family whose four-year-old indigo daughter was regularly beating up their one-year-old baby. I spoke of past life issues with them and they shut down completely. Instead, they went to traditional Western helpers. If they did not succeed there, one or both of their children could end up being apprehended by child protection services.

You need to decide how important it is to you to resolve your difficulties and what your highest priority is – your beliefs or your well-being and that of your child. You don't need to believe what I say, but simply be open to trying something different if your current solutions aren't working.

My suggestion when nothing else works: ask for help and trust in Spirit, and surrender to higher guidance. If this is difficult for you, ask for guidance from someone who can help to broaden your perspective on your dilemma, in terms that include a focus on your spirit. We're given our challenges to push us to grow beyond our limitations and beyond our ego to connect more and more fully with Spirit. I recommend that you take full advantage of your difficulties to go further and further in your growth. My goal is simply to show you some methods and a path that have proven to be very effective with many indigos and other sensitive souls and their families.

As for me, getting beat up by various types of negativity over time has been invaluable, although I don't recommend it to anyone. These experiences not only helped me to grow tremendously, but in mastering them for myself, I'm able to assist more and more people who haven't been helped by other methods. I'm now able to teach these methods so that more and more people can help others and transform their own lives for the better. I believe that everything is part of God / Spirit / Creator, and therefore all is good. Negativity is simply an opportunity to help us grow.

As I said at the beginning of this book, it's useful to remember the Zen perspective that what we need to focus on is to keep the mirror of our consciousness clean – keep brushing off negativity as it shows up.

We need to plan for the future and heal the past, but our focus needs to be on the present - and transform whatever comes up for us and our children with a gentle compassionate touch. It's our chosen path and our will that takes us from one point to another. I recommend to you the path of service rather than that of avoiding pain and increasing material pleasures. Self-serving does not work well for old souls and indigos, or for other sensitive souls. Because they're advanced souls, they have little choice but to serve, although many haven't realized that yet.

We also need to remember that we're all already in the light – we've just forgotten. We need to be healed and assisted to remember. We already have Christ consciousness, Buddha nature, Krishna consciousness. We just need to remove the obstacles.

And what we see as negativity is either an opportunity to resolve old karma, to pay for old sins so to speak, or lessons from the universe to teach us what we need to learn. That needs to be balanced with walking away from abusive situations and people when it goes too far. This is the balance between surrender and being in our power to protect ourselves and our children, and to serve.

In summary, the bottom line is to serve Spirit and to gradually go closer and closer to the Godhead. To be more and more full with Spirit, until we eventually become one with God. And serve others in the process. Put that in your own terms and go for it.

Namaste – I salute the light within you.

Bibliography

Ahrons, C. The Good Divorce. New York, NY: HarperCollins, 1994.

American Heart Association. Alert: Overweight Children. http://www.americanheart.org/presenter. jhtml?identifier=4670. Downloaded December 29, 2009.

Andrews, D. Criminal Behaviour: A Collection of Readings. Self-published, 1982.

Aron, E. The Highly Sensitive Child. New York, NY: Broadway Books, 2002.

Aron, E. The Highly Sensitive Person. New York, NY: Broadway Books, 1996.

Atkinson, B. Emotional Intelligence in Couples Therapy: Advances from Neurobiology and the Science of Intimate Relationships. New York, NY: W.W. Norton & Company, 2005.

Atwater, P. Beyond the Indigo Children: The New Children and the Coming of the Fifth World. Rochester, VT: Bear & Company, 2005.

Austin, S., Haines, J., and Veugelers, P. Body satisfaction and body weight: Gender differences and sociodemographic determinants. BMC Public Health, 2009, 9, 313.

Barkley, R. Taking Charge of ADHD: The Complete, Authoritative Guide for Parents. New York, NY: The Guilford Press, 1995.

Barkley, R. and Benton, C. Your Defiant Child: Eight Steps to Better Behavior. New York, NY: The Guildford Press, 1998.

Belli, B. Guarding against autism: How environmental toxins may contribute to autism spectrum disorder. Natural Awakenings, San Diego Edition, January, 2010, pp.22-23. Available at http://www.na-sd.com/.

Benor, D. Seven Minutes to Natural Pain Release. Santa Ross, CA: Energy Psychology Press, 2008.

Blackburn Losey, M. The Children of Now: Crystalline Children, Indigo Children, Star Kids, Angels on Earth, and the Phenomenon of Transitional Children. Franklin, NJ: New Page Books, 2007.

Blackburn Losey, M. Parenting the Children of Now. San Francisco, CA: Weiser Books, 2009.

Blofeld, J. The Zen Teachings of Huang Po: On the Transmission of Mind. Berkeley, CA: Shambhala, 1994.

Bowlby, J. Attachment and Loss, Volume 1: Attachment. New York, NY: Basic Books, 1969.

Bradshaw, J. Healing the Shame that Binds You. Deerfield Beach, FL: Health Communications, 1988.

Bradshaw, J. Homecoming: Reclaiming and Championing Your Inner Child. New York, NY: Bantam Books, 1990.

Burger, J. The Gaia Atlas of First Peoples. New York, NY: Anchor Books, 1990.

Burns, D. Feeling Good: The New Mood Therapy. New York, NY: HarperCollins, 1999.

Callaghan, R. and Trubo, R. Tapping the Healer Within: Using Thought-Field Therapy to Instantly Conquer Your Fears, Anxieties, and Emotional Distress. Toronto, ON: McGraw-Hill, 2002.

Canetti, L., Bachar, E., Galili-Weisstub, E., Kaplan De-Nour, A., and Shalev, A. Parental bonding and mental health in adolescence. Adolescence, 1997, 32, 117-133.

Carrion, V., Weems, C., and Reiss, A. Stress predicts brain changes in children. Pediatrics, 2007, 119, 509-516.

Carroll, L. and Tober, J. The Indigo Children: The New Kids Have Arrived. Carlsbad, CA: Hay House, 1999.

Carroll, L. and Tober, J. An Indigo Celebration: More Messages, Stories, and Insights from the Indigo Children. Carlsbad, CA: Hay House, 2001.

Carroll, L. and Tober, J. The Indigo Children Ten Years Later: What's Happening with the Indigo Teenagers! Carlsbad, CA: Hay House, 2009.

Carter, B. and McGoldrick, M. The Expanded Family Life Cycle: Individual, Family, and Social Perspectives. White Plains, NY: Allyn & Bacon, 2005.

Caserta, M. Stressed parents equals sick kids. New Scientist, March 2008, 2648.

Cassidy, J. and Shaver, P. (Eds.) Handbook of Attachment Theory, Research, and Clinical Applications. New York, NY: The Guilford Press, 1999.

Chodron, P. No Time to Lose: A Timely Guide to the Way of the Bodhisattva. Berkeley, CA: Shambhala, 2005.

Chopra, D. Jesus: A Story of Enlightenment. New York, NY: HarperCollins, 2008.

Course in Miracles. Tiburon, CA: Foundation for Inner Peace, 1975.

Craig, G. EFT. www.emofree.com.

De Bellis, M. The psychobiology of neglect. Child Maltreatment, 2005, 10, 2, 150-172.

de Shazer, S. Keys to Solution in Brief Therapy. New York, NY: W.W. Norton & Company, 1985.

Di Buono, M. Heart and Stroke Report on the Health of Ontario's Kids. Ottawa, ON: Heart and Stroke Foundation, 2009.

de Chardin, T. The Future of Man. Dorset, England: Image, 2004.

Dosick, W. and Dosick, E. Spiritually Healing the Indigo Children (and Adult Indigos, Too!): The Practical Guide and Handbook. San Diego, CA: Jodere Group, 2004.

Dosick, W. and Dosick, E. Empowering Your Indigo Child: A Handbook for Parents of Children of Spirit. San Francisco, CA: Red Wheel/Weiser 2009.

Dossey, L. Prayer Is Good Medicine: How to Reap the Healing Benefits of Prayer. New York, NY: HarperCollins, 1997.

American Psychiatric Association: DSM–IV-TR. Washington, DC: American Psychiatric Association, 2000.

Eisler, I., Dare, C., Hodes, M., Russell, G., Dodge, E., and Le Grange, D. Family therapy for adolescent anorexia nervosa: The results of a controlled comparison of two family interventions. Journal of Child Psychology and Psychiatry. 2000, 41(6), 727-736.

Eisler, I., Le Grange, D., and Asen, K. Family interventions. In J. Treasure (Ed.), Handbook of Eating Disorders. 2nd edition. Chichester, England: Wiley, 2003, pp. 291–310.

Ellis, A. and Harper, R. A Guide to Rational Living. Chatsworth, CA: Wilshire Book Co., 1975.

Emerton, K. Involved fathers key for children. http://www. eurekalert.org/pub_releases/2002-03/esr-ifk030102.php. Downloaded April 21, 2010.

Feinstein, D. Energy psychology in disaster relief. Traumatology, 2008, 14, 1, 127-139.

Felsen, I. Transgenerational transmission of effects of the Holocaust. In Y. Danieli (Ed.), International Handbook of Multigenerational Legacies of Trauma. New York, NY: Plenum Press, 1998.

Fidelman, C. Mother's touch has the power to heal. Montreal Gazette, 2009, Apr. 24, 2008.

Figley, C. Treating Compassion Fatigue. New York, NY: Routledge, 2002.

Figley, C. Compassion Fatigue: Coping with Secondary Traumatic Stress Disorder in Those Who Treat the Traumatized. New York, NY: Brunner/Mazel, 1995.

Freud, A. The Ego and the Mechanisms of Defense. New Haven, CT: International Universities Press, 1967.

Freud, S. The Ego and the Id. New York, NY: W.W. Norton & Company, 1923.

Gerrig, R. and Zimbardo, P. Psychology and Life, 18th edition. Boston, MA: Allyn & Bacon, 2008.

Godman, D. Be as You Are: The Teachings of Sri Ramana Maharshi. New York, NY: Routledge, 1985.

Goleman, D. Emotional Intelligence. New York, NY: Bantam, 1995.

Goleman, D. Destructive Emotions: How Can We Overcome Them? A Scientific Dialogue with the Dalai Lama. New York, NY: Bantam, 2003.

Goleman, D. Social Intelligence. New York, NY: Bantam, 2006.

Goode, C. and Paterson, T. Raising Intuitive Children: Guide Your Children to Know and Trust their Gifts. Franklin Lakes, NJ: New Page Books, 2009.

Gottman, J. Raising an Emotionally Intelligent Child: The Heart of Parenting. New York, NY: Fireside, 1997.

Harris, T. I'm OK - You're OK. New York, NY: Avon, 1976.

Greenhouse, S. The Big Squeeze: Tough Times for the American Worker. New York, NY: Knopf, 2008.

Haley, J. Problem-Solving Therapy. San Francisco, CA: Jossey-Bass, 1987.

Harding, C. Remission vs. recovery: Two very different concepts. Conference presentation at Reclaiming Lives: What Professionals Need to Know About Assessment, Planning, and Treatment for People Who Appear to be Stuck on the Road to Recovery, Boston University Center for

Psychiatric Rehabilitation at the Sargent College of Health and Rehabilitation Sciences, April 13, 2004.

Hawkes, J. Cell-Level Healing: The Bridge from Soul to Cell. New York, NY: Atria Books/Beyond Words, 2006.

Heart and Stroke Report on the Health of Ontario's Children, as reported on CTV News, Sept. 9, 2009.

Hawkins, D. Power vs. Force: The Hidden Determinants of Human Behavior. Carlsbad, CA: Hay House, 1995.

Hawkins, D. I: Reality and Subjectivity. Carlsbad, CA: Hay House, 2003.

Hawkins, D. Transcending the Levels of Consciousness. Carlsbad, CA: Hay House, 2006.

Hawkins, S., Cole, T., and Law, C. Examining the relationship between maternal employment and health behaviours in 5-year-old British children. Journal of Epidemiology and Community Health. 2009, 63, 999, online.

Henderson, M., Hotopf, M., and Leon, D. Childhood temperament and long-term sickness absence in adult life. British Journal of Psychiatry, 2009, 194, 220-223.

Henggeler, S., Schoenwald, S., Borduin, C., Rowland, M., and Cunningham, P. Multisystemic Treatment of Antisocial Behavior in Children and Adolescents. New York, NY: The Guilford Press, 1998.

Higgins, E. Do ADHD drugs take a toll on the brain? Scientific American Mind. July/August 2009, pp. 39-43.

Jaffe, K. and Davidson, R. Indigo Adults: Forerunners of the New Civilization. Lincoln, NE: iUniverse, 2005.

Johnson, S. Hold Me Tight: Seven Conversations for a Lifetime of Love. New York, NY: Little, Brown and Company, 2008.

Kazdin, A. The Kazdin Method for Parenting the Defiant Child: With No Pills, No Therapy, No Contest of Wills. New York, NY: Houghton Mifflin Company, 2008.

King, S. and Ballard, R. KIDS! Indigo Children & Cheeky Monkeys. Glen Waverley, Australia: Blue Angel Gallery, 2008.

Kolari, J. Connected Parenting: Transform Your Challenging Child and Build Loving Bonds for Life. New York, NY: Viking, 2009.

Lao Tsu. Tao Te Ching. New York, NY: Vintage, 1972.

Lancaster, D. Anger and the Indigo Child. Boulder, CO: Wellness Press, 2002.

Lennon, J. Crippled Inside, Album – Imagine, 1971.

Levine, P. Waking the Tiger: Healing Trauma. Berkeley, CA: North Atlantic Books, 1997.

Levine, S. and Levine, O. Embracing the Beloved: Relationship as a Path of Awakening. Toronto, ON: Anchor Books, 1995.

Levav, I. Kohn, R., and Schwartz, S. The psychiatric after-effects of the Holocaust on the second generation. Psychological Medicine, 1998, 28, 755-760.

Levy, T. and Orlans, M. Attachment, Trauma, and Healing: Understanding and Treating Attachment Disorder in Children and Families. Washington, DC: CWLA Press, 1998.

Liddle, H. Multidimensional family therapy for adolescent cannabis users. (Cannabis Youth Treatment Series, Vol. 5). Rockville, MD: Center for Substance Abuse Treatment, 2002.

McGowan, P., Sasaki, A., D'Alessio, A., Dymov, S., Labonté, B., Szyf, M., Turecki, G., and Meany, M. Epigenetic regulation of the glucocorticoid receptor in human brain associated with childhood abuse. Nature Neuroscience, 2009, 12, 342-348.

McTaggart, Lynne. The Intention Experiment. New York, NY: Free Press, 2007.

McTaggart, Lynne. What Doctors Don't Tell You: The Truth About the Dangers of Modern Medicine. New York, NY: Avon Books, 1996.

Maiberger, B. EMDR Essentials: A Guide for Clients and Therapists. London, England: W.W. Norton & Company, 2009.

Maltz, M. Psycho-Cybernetics. New York, NY: Pocket, 1989.

Madanes, C. Strategic Family Therapy. San Francisco, CA: Jossey-Bass, 1981.

Mash, E. and Barkley, R. Child Psychopathology. New York, NY: The Guilford Press, 2003.

Maté, G. Scattered Minds: A New Look at the Origins and Healing of Attention Deficit Disorder. Toronto, ON: Knopf, 2000.

Maté, G. In the Realms of the Hungry Ghosts: Close Encounters with Addiction. Toronto, ON: Knopf, 2008.

Minuchin, S. Family Therapy Techniques. Cambridge, MA: Harvard University Press, 1981.

Minuchin, S., Rosman, B., and Baker, L. Psychosomatic Families: Anorexia Nervosa in Context. Cambridge, MA: Harvard University Press, 1978.

Moore, M. Capitalism: A Love Story. Film, 2009.

Nagata, D. International effects of the Japanese American internment. In Y. Danieli (Ed.), International Handbook of Multigenerational Legacies of Trauma. New York, NY: Plenum Press, 1998.

Naparstek, B. Staying Well with Guided Imagery. New York, NY: Warner Books, 1994.

Neufeld, G. and Maté, G. Hold On to Your Kids: Why Parents Need to Matter More Than Peers. Toronto, ON: Vintage, 2004.

Newton, M. Journey of Souls video at http://www.youtube. com/watch?v=NQ99V8s5qfE.

Newton, M. Journey of Souls: Case Studies of Life Between Lives. Woodbury, MN: Llewellyn Publications, 1994.

Nithyananda, P. Living Enlightenment. Bangalore, India: Life Bliss Foundation, 2008.

Ornish, D. Love and Survival: The Scientific Basis for the Healing Power of Intimacy. New York, NY: HarperCollins, 1998.

Paiton, M. Encouraging Your Child's Spiritual Intelligence. New York, NY: Atria Books/Beyond Words, 2007.

Patanjali: How to Know God: The Yoga Aphorisms of Patanjali. New York, NY: Mentor, 1953.

Patillo, N. Children of the Stars. Huntsville, AR: Ozark Mountain Publishing, 2008.

Pearlman, L. and Saakvitne, K. Transforming the Pain: A Workbook on Vicarious Traumatization. New York, NY: W.W. Norton & Company, 1996.

Pearlman, L. Vicarious traumatization: An empirical study of the effects of trauma work on trauma therapists. Professional Psychology: Research and Practice, 1995, Dec. 26 (6), 558-565.

Pemberton, K. Violence in the Classroom. The Vancouver Sun, March 27, 2010, p. 1.

Perera, F., Li, Z., Whyatt, R., Hoepner, L., Wang, S., Camann, D., and Rauh, V. Prenatal airborne polycyclic aromatic hydrocarbon exposure and child IQ at age 5 years. Pediatrics, 2009, 10, 1542, 2008-3506.

Pope, J. The World According to Michael: An Old Soul's Guide to the Universe. Fayette, AZ: Emerald Wave, 1992.

Prabhupada, A. Bhagavad-Gita As It Is. Singapore: Bhaktivedanta Book Trust, 2006.

Pruett, K. Fatherneed: Why Father Care Is as Essential as Mother Care for Your Child. New York, NY: Free Press, 2000.

Rogers, C. On Becoming a Person: A Therapist's View of Psychotherapy. Boston, MA: Mariner Books, 1995.

Rossman, M. Guided Imagery for Self-Healing. Tiburon, CA: H.J. Kramer Books, 2000.

Ralph, R. Review of the recovery literature: Synthesis of a sample recovery literature 2000. National Association for State Mental Health Program Directors. Downloaded Oct. 11, 2009.

Ray, P. and Anderson, S. The Cultural Creatives: How 50 Million People Are Changing the World. New York, NY: Crown Publishing Group, 2001.

Rosack, J. New data add to puzzle about antidepressant, youth-suicide link. Psychiatric News, 2006, 41, 17, 2.

Ruiz, D. The Four Agreements. San Rafael, CA: Amber-Allen Publishing, 1997.

Santrock, J. Adolescence. Toronto, ON: McGraw-Hill, 2009.

Sauvé, R. The Current State of Family Finances. Ottawa: The Vanier Institute, 2010.

Sax, L. Why Gender Matters: What Parents and Teachers Need to Know About the Emerging Science of Sex Differences. New York, NY: Broadway Books, 2006.

Sax, L. Boys Adrift: The Five Factors Driving the Growing Epidemic of Unmotivated Boys and Underachieving Young Men. New York, NY: Broadway Books, 2009.

Sax, L. Girls on the Edge: The Four Factors Driving the New Crisis for Girls - Sexual Identity, the Cyberbubble, Obsessions, Environmental Toxins. New York, NY: Basic Books, 2010.

Schulz, M. Awakening Intuition: Using Your Mind-Body Network for Insight and Healing. New York, NY: Three Rivers Press, 1998.

Sexton, T. and Alexander, J. Functional Family Therapy, 2010, http://www.ncjrs.gov/pdffiles1/ojjdp/184743.pdf.

Sexton, T. and Alexander, J. Functional family therapy. In T. Patterson (Ed.), Comprehensive Handbook of Psychotherapy, Volume II. New York, NY: Wiley, 2002.

Shapiro, F. EMDR: The Breakthrough Therapy for Overcoming Anxiety, Stress, and Trauma. New York, NY: Basic Books, 1997.

Siegel, D. and Hartzell, M. Parenting from the Inside Out. New York, NY: Penguin, 2003.

Siegel, D. The Developing Mind: Toward a Neurobiology of Interpersonal Experience. New York, NY: The Guilford Press, 1999.

Solomon, Z. Transgenerational effects of the Holocaust. In Y. Danieli (Ed.), International Handbook of Multigenerational Legacies of Trauma. New York, NY: Plenum Press, 1998.

Spangler, D. Parent as Mystic, Mystic as Parent. New York, NY: Riverhead, 1998.

Spock, B. Doctor Spock's Baby and Child Care. New York, NY: NYU Press, 2005.

Springen, K. Daring to die. Scientific American Mind, 2010, January, pp. 40-47.

St. Jean, I. Living Forward, Giving Back: A Practical Guide to Fulfillment in Midlife and Beyond. Vancouver, Canada: Inspired Momentum, 2008.

Stone, J. Soul Psychology: How to Clear Negative Emotions and Spiritualize Your Life. New York, NY: Ballantine Wellspring, 1994.

Lama Surya Das. Buddha Is As Buddha Does: The Ten Original Practices for Enlightened Living. San Francisco, CA: HarperCollins, 2007.

Szapocznik, J. and Williams, R. Brief strategic family therapy. Clinical Child and Family Psychology Review, 2000, 3, 2, 117-134.

Tanous, A. and Donnelly, K. Is Your Child Psychic?: A Guide to Developing Your Child's Innate Abilities. New York, NY: Penguin, 1979.

Thivierge, R., Thompson, D., and Carter, C. The Effectiveness of a Family Therapy Program in a Child Welfare Context. Unpublished manuscript, 1988.

Thivierge, R. Being a Positive Resource to Child Welfare Families. Unpublished manuscript, 1995.

Thivierge, R. Out of Bed & Into the Fire: Damage Control During Relationship Breakdown. Vancouver, BC: Phoenix Vision, 2006.

Tolin, D. and Foa, E. Sex differences in trauma and post traumatic stress disorder: A quantitative review of 25 years of research. Psychological Bulletin, 2006, 132, 959-992.

Tremblay, M. Active Healthy Kids Canada. https://www.lib.uwo.ca/blogs/education/2009/08/active-healthy-kids-canada-web.html. Downloaded March 2010.

Thondup, T. Boundless Healing: Meditation Exercises to Enlighten the Mind and Heal the Body. Berkeley, CA: Shambhala, 2000.

Twyman, J. Messages from Thomas: Raising Psychic Children. Findhorn, Scotland: Findhorn Press, 2003.

Tytell, T. Trauma and its aftermath: A differentiated picture of the aftereffects of trauma in daughters of Holocaust survivors. Dissertation Abstracts International, 1999, 59, 4490.

Vitale, J. and Len, I. Zero Limits: The Secret Hawaiian System for Wealth, Health, Peace, and More. Hoboken, NJ: John Wiley & Sons, 2008.

Virtue, D. The Care and Feeding of Indigo Children. Carlsbad, CA: Hay House, 2001.

Virtue, D. The Crystal Children. Carlsbad, CA: Hay House, 2003.

Virtue, D. Indigo, Crystal, and Rainbow Children. Carlsbad, CA: Hay House, 2005. Compact disc.

Wangyal Rinpoche, T. Healing with Form, Energy, and Light: The Five Elements in Tibetan Shamanism, Tantra, and Dzogchen. Ithaca, NY: Snow Lion, 2002.

Warren, R. The Purpose Driven Life. Grand Rapids, MI: Zondervan, 2002.

Wikipedia: Anorexia.
http://en.wikipedia.org/wiki/Anorexia_nervosa.

Winnicott, D. W. Mirror-role of the mother and family in child development. In P. Lomas (Ed.), The Predicament of the Family: A Psycho-Analytical Symposium. London: Hogarth, 1967, 26-33.

Winnicott, W. Psycho-Analytic Explorations. Cambridge, MA: Harvard University Press. 1989.

Wyman, P., Moynihan, J., Eberly, S., Cox, C., Cress, W., Jin, X., and Caserta, M. Association of family stress with natural killer cell activity and the frequency of illnesses in children. Archives Pediatric Adolescent Medicine. 2007, 61, 228-234.

Youth on Drugs: Effects, Warnings, Treatment. http://www. vancouversun.com/health/Just+doesn+work+students+behi nd+anti+drug+website/2905308/story.html.

CPSIA information can be obtained
at www.ICGtesting.com
Printed in the USA
BVHW041154280820
587548BV00014B/462